Contemporary
COOKING

Volume 11

Contemporary
COOKING

Volume 11

3M

Contemporary Cooking

© Marshall Cavendish Ltd. 1983
© Minnesota Mining & Mfg. Co. 1985

Editorial production by James Charlton Associates, Ltd., New York. Editor-in-Chief, James Charlton; Executive Editor, Cara DeSilva; Managing Editors, Barbara Binswanger, Jennie McGregor; Food Editors, Gilda Abramowitz, Helen Feingold, Judy Knipe, Inez M. Krech, Betsy Lawrence, Anne Lanigan, Maria Robbins, Susan Sarao, Joan Whitman; Wine Consultant, Rory Callahan.

Book production and manufacturing consulting by: Cobb/Dunlop Publishing Services, Inc., New York Art Direction and interior design by: Marsha Cohen/Parallelogram Layout by: Jeanne Borczuk of SOHO Studio, New York Composition by: Kachina Typesetting, Tempe, Arizona Cover design by: Koechel/Peterson Design, Minneapolis

Acknowledgments: Pat Cocklin, Delu PAL International, Alan Duns, John Elliott, Gus Francisco Photography, Melvin Grey, Gina Harris, Anthony Kay, Paul Kemp, David Levin, David Meldrum, Roger Phillips, Nick Powell, Iain Reid, John Turner, Paul Williams, George Wright, Cuisinarts, Inc.

Printed and bound in Yugoslavia by CGP Delo.

Library of Congress Cataloging in Publication Data
Main entry under title:

Contemporary Cooking.

  Includes index.
  1. Cookery. I. Minnesota Mining and Manufacturing
Company.
TX715.C7586   1984   641.5   84-2563
0-88159-500-4 — (set)
ISBN: 0-88159–010–X

CONTENTS
for the Contemporary Cooking Series

VOLUME 11

Part One

CHEESE AND CHEESEMAKING

A cheese may disappoint. It may be dull, it may be naive, it may be oversophisticated. Yet it remains cheese, milk's leap toward immortality.

—Clifton Fadiman

Leave a container of milk out too long and the solid parts, the curd (containing most of the proteins and fat), will separate from the thinner, watery parts (the whey) and what you've got is an evil-smelling lot of spoiled milk. Ironically, what you also have is the crude beginnings of cheese—one of the longest keeping, most nutritious, varied and tasty items in the culinary cornucopia. Of course, it has been six thousand years or more since some brave soul, whether out of curiosity or hunger, decided to go ahead and eat the "spoiled" milk. In the meantime, cheese making has become both an art and a science of infinite subtlety.

When curds are simply separated from the whey, what results is a relatively simple comestible called fresh cheese. But the curds really come into their own as unique cheeses when they are subjected to any combination of thousands of curing methods. The curing may include controlled exposure to various fungi and bacteria, heating, mixing, drying, salting, pressing, molding, flavoring and, finally, aging. The precise and specific combination of these and other variables will determine the nature of the cheese that results.

The cheese maker's mainstay is a substance called rennet, found in the stomachs of unweaned calves, kids and other mammals. Rennet has the property of dramatically speeding up the curdling process. In fact, its effect is so powerful that one gallon of it will curdle a million gallons of whole milk. Early Middle Eastern shepherds had a habit of carrying their day's supply of milk in flasks made of sheep or goat intestine. It was probably the naturally occurring rennet in the flask that created the first batch of true cheese.

In any case, cheese has certainly had a long, glorious and varied history since that time, and its sustaining nutritional value seems to have been well understood from very early on. Mentioned several times in the Bible, it was cheese (or at least the need to deliver ten large loaves of it to the embattled armies of Saul) that brought David to his confrontation with Goliath. Cheese was also well known and much loved in ancient Greece. Homer mentions that the Cyclops, Polyphemus, was a maker of cheese, and Olympic athletes are known to have trained on a special diet that consisted largely of cheese.

In Roman times it was said that the prophet Zoroaster had subsisted in the desert for twenty years on a single variety of cheese, though in Rome at least, a wide variety was already available from the far-flung corners of the empire. Indeed, when the Romans arrived in England they found the inhabitants of the place now known as Chester producing a locally famous cheese not unlike the world-famous Cheshire cheese that is still produced there. The Romans were so taken with it that they fortified the town just to insure an uninterrupted supply. (Incidentally, Cheshire cheese was traditionally made in odd-shaped molds, some in the form of cats—no doubt the inspiration for Lewis Carroll's grinning tabby.)

In the Dark Ages it was the monasteries, those industrious preservers of craft and knowledge, that were ideally suited to the pastoral but labor-intensive job of cheese making—at first for their own consumption, but later in sufficient quantity for substantial commerce. It is said that it was the monks of Saint Gall who gave Charlemagne his first taste of Roquefort cheese, though they were forced to tell the Holy Roman Emperor, as diplomatically as possible, no doubt, that by avoiding the green veins he was depriving himself of the best parts. The Great Charles was so pleased with the cheese that he put in a standing order for two cartloads a year.

In the centuries that followed, the techniques of cheese making changed little, though the introduction or discovery of a new variety was always a cause for local celebration and pride. Many cheeses, by virtue of their superior or unique qualities, achieved international prominence. Napoleon is said to have jumped to his feet to kiss the lowly serving girl who first offered him Camembert, and in 1815 the princely Congress of Vienna interrupted its political concerns to herald Brie as the cheese of kings.

Queen Victoria's coronation was commemorated with a cheese of more than a thousand pounds, and monumentally sized cheeses have been lending their festive, if somewhat daunting, presence to special events for centuries. The ultimate in this tradition (one hopes) was the seventeen-ton specimen presented at the 1964–1965 World's Fair in New York.

Modern times brought pressures to produce larger quantities of cheese by modern methods, though such efforts have often failed when the inherent wisdom of the traditional methods were not adequately respected. A Swiss-American named Emil Frey learned that lesson the hard way. In 1889, working out of a small ramshackle facility in upstate New York, Frey invented a new cheese that he called Liederkranz, in honor of a glee club of that name to which he belonged. The cheese was (and still is) a big success, and demand for it grew rapidly. Before long Frey moved his operation into a large, new and immaculate building in Ohio, where he felt he would be assured of a greater supply of fresh milk. The cheese he produced, however, was nearly tasteless—a far cry from the pungently delicious product he had made in New York. His company was nearing disaster until a bright employee thought to fetch back from New York the filthy, encrusted drying shelves that had been left behind. The accumulated mold and crud were scraped from the shelves and smeared all over the pristine walls of the new facility, and Frey was back in business.

These days Americans have access to more varieties of cheese than ever before and have once again begun, like their forefathers and -mothers, to experiment with making their own.

The miracle of cheese is that by controlling the circumstances under which milk spoils, we preserve it, transforming, in the process, this most fundamental of nourishments into a food of infinitely variable taste and texture, from the innocuously mild to the breathtakingly malodorous. It goes without saying that between those extremes there remains a world of gustatory delight for every palate.

CHEESES

What is cheese? A cheese is simply milk that has been set to curd and then is drained partly or wholly of its whey by pressing or heating or both. (Sometimes the whey is reserved and eaten—remember Little Miss Muffet; sometimes the whey alone is made into a cheese.) All cheese is based on milk, whether it is from the cow, water buffalo, goat, or sheep. Over the centuries, many different varieties of cheese have been invented. They can range from very soft to hard, buttery to very sharp, smooth to granular.

There are several categories in which to classify cheese. These are not strict, as one cheese at a different age may be in two of the categories.

• Very hard cheeses, such as Romano, Parmesan and Sapsago, are best for grating.

• Hard cheeses, such as Cheddar, Emmental and Gruyère, are very good for cooking.

• Semisoft cheeses, such as brick, muenster, Limburger, Port-Salut and blue cheeses, are especially good table cheeses.

• Soft cheeses that are ripened, such as Brie, Camembert and French Neufchâtel, are also very good table cheeses. Unripened soft cheeses, such as pot, cottage, cream and ricotta, are good for table use or in cooking.

As you will see in the recipes that follow, it is not necessary to cook cheese to combine it with other flavors. Cheese is a very versatile food: It can be eaten at breakfast with bread, fruit, or eggs; at lunch it can be part of a sandwich or a more elaborate preparation; at dinner it can be served as a tasty appetizer or combined with fruit and crackers and served as an elegant end to the meal; and, of course, it is a nutritious snack food.

Cheese Varieties

The cheeses that are described below are merely an introduction to the world of cheese. The United States Department of Agriculture lists more than 400 varieties of cheeses from around the world.

Appenzell—A cow's-milk cheese from Switzerland. Before aging, it is soaked in a mixture of cider or white wine and spices.

Asiago—A pungent cow's-milk cheese made in various northern regions of Italy. Like other matured grating cheeses, it may be eaten as a table cheese when young.

Bel Paese—An Italian semisoft cow's-milk cheese with a smooth rind.

Blue Cheese—America's blue-veined cheese, made from cow's or goat's milk.

Brick—This semisoft but pungent cheese was first made in Wisconsin. It has many irregular holes, but slices well.

Brie—The queen of the French soft-ripened cheeses. Made from cow's milk, Brie is similar to Camembert in that they both are ripened, in part, by molds and bacteria that grow on the surface of the cheese.

Bucheron—A tangy, creamy chèvre (see below).

Caerphilly—A mild, white, crumbly-textured cow's-milk table cheese from England and Wales.

Camembert—Like Brie, Camembert is a soft, surface-ripened cow's-milk cheese with a center that is creamy when ripe. When overripe it has a strong ammoniated smell.

Capra—A smooth, delicately flavored goat's-milk cheese from Italy.

Cheddar—An English cheese named for a village in Somerset, where it was first made. Cheddar is a hard cow's-milk cheese, ranging in color from almost white to bright orange, and in taste from mild to very sharp. Sixty-seven percent of all Cheddar is now made in the United States.

Cheshire—A hard, crumbly cow's-milk cheese similar to Cheddar. Once molded to look like the famous Cheshire Cat.

Chèvre—The French word for "goat" as well as goat cheese.

Colby—A semisoft, open-textured cow's-milk cheese with a mild flavor.

Coon—A Cheddar cheese that is cured by a special patented method. It has a dark color and is very crumbly. Similar to a extra-sharp Cheddar.

Cottage—Sometimes called pot cheese or Dutch cheese, this is a soft, white, uncured cow's-milk cheese.

Cream—A soft, mild, rich, uncured cheese made from cream or a mixture of cream and milk. It is similar to Neufchâtel, but has a higher fat content.

Crottin de Chavignol—A tiny goat cheese from the French province of Berry, it is soft and mild when fresh and hard and sharp when aged.

Danbo—A mild, semisoft Danish cheese that is sometimes made with caraway seeds.

Derby—A hard, delicate-tasting curd cheese from England, made from cow's milk. It is similar to Cheddar but not as hard. Sage Derby has fine green veins of sage running through it.

Edam—A semisoft to hard cheese from the Netherlands, made from whole cow's milk. It has a mild, sometimes salty flavor and a close, elastic texture.

Emmental—A semisoft cow's-milk cheese with a mellow flavor. Probably the most imitated cheese in the world, this is genuine Swiss cheese. Look for the name "Switzerland" repeatedly stamped on the rind.

Farmer—A soft curd cheese similar to cottage. It is usually molded and sold in blocks.

Feta—A white pickled goat's, sheep's, or cow's-milk cheese from Greece with a firm texture and a salty flavor.

Fontina—A semisoft to hard cheese from Italy, with a sweet nutty flavor.

Gjetöst—Originally a goat's-milk cheese, now commonly made from a mixture of cow's and goat's milk. It is caramel-colored and actually made with sugar, but tastes like any other cheese.

Gloucester—A hard cow's-milk cheese, with a mild but full flavor. Rich and creamy Double Gloucester is

Cheese Varieties

Appenzell

Blue Cheese

Brie

Bucheron

Cheddar

Crottin de Chavignol

Danbo

Emmental

Feta

Cheese Varieties (continued)

Gjetöst

Gloucester

Gouda

Manchego

Mascarpone

Mozzarella

Parmesan

Port-Salut

Saint André

made with twice the amount of milk and is one of England's greats.

Gorgonzola—The principal blue-veined cheese of Italy and one of the most famous cheeses in the world. Creamier than Roquefort.

Gouda—A semisoft to hard cow's-milk cheese, similar to Edam with higher fat content. The surface is often coated with red wax. Aged Gouda, when farmhouse produced, can be extraordinarily fine.

Gruyère—Produced in Switzerland or France, Gruyère is made in a similar manner to Emmental, but it has smaller holes and a sharper flavor. Like Emmental, it is a cow's-milk cheese.

Havarti—A Danish cow's-milk cheese with an open texture and a mild to sharp flavor, depending on age.

Jarlsberg—A Swiss-type cow's-milk cheese from Norway, Jarlsberg has a mild and nutty flavor. It has become very popular in the United States.

Kasseri—This Greek sheep's-milk cheese is hard, white, and mild-tasting.

Kuminost—Made in the Scandinavian countries, this Colby type of cow's-milk cheese is flavored with cumin, caraway and other spices.

Lancashire—This English cow's-milk cheese is similar to Cheddar and Cheshire, but it has a softer, more crumbly texture and, as it ages, a stronger flavor.

Liederkranz—A soft, surface-ripened cheese made in the United States. It has a strong aroma and flavor and was modeled after Limburger cheese.

Limburger—A semisoft cow's-milk cheese with a particularly pungent smell and taste. Originally from Belgium but strongly associated with Germany, where it is widely made and eaten.

Manchego—One of the best cheeses of Spain, it is renowned for being exceptionally nourishing. It is made from sheep's milk and, depending on its age, can range from mild but distinctive to quite sharp and unmistakable.

Mascarpone—A very soft cow's-milk cream cheese from Italy. It is similar to fresh ricotta in consistency and has a buttery, mildly acidic flavor. Frequently served with fruit.

Montrachet—One of the most popular of the French goat cheeses. It is cylinder-shaped and frequently covered with ash.

Monterey Jack—This semisoft cheese is made in the United States from whole or skimmed cow's milk. There is also a dry, aged version, most often used for grating.

Mozzarella—A soft delicate-tasting cheese that was originally made only from the milk of the water buffalo, but is now most commonly made from cow's milk. Buy as fresh as possible and never confuse real mozzarella with the rubbery variation commonly thought of as pizza cheese. Real mozzarella is always available smoked.

Muenster—A semisoft whole-milk cheese, similar to brick.

Neufchâtel—In its fresh state, a soft, mild cow's-milk cheese from France. It is also sometimes cured, in heart-shaped or cylindrical molds, and then acquires a much tangier taste. American-made Neufchâtel is very similar to our cream cheese, but has a lower fat content.

Noekkelost—A Norwegian spiced cheese, similar to Kuminost. Cumin, cloves and caraway are the spices most often used.

Oka—A semisoft cow's-milk cheese made by Trappist monks in a monastery near Oka, Quebec. It is similar to Port-Salut.

Parmesan—Although this is the name commonly employed outside Italy for a group of very hard cow's-milk cheeses, the only real Parmesan is Parmigiano-Reggiano, which by law must come from the areas of Parma and Reggio Emilia. This great cheese is the color of straw, has a nutty, salty flavor, and is delicious both as a table cheese and for grating. A real Parmesan will always have the name Parmigiano-Reggiano stamped all over the rind. Check before you buy.

Pont l'Evêque—A soft cow's-milk cheese from Normandy, with a distinct tangy taste.

Port-Salut—This cow's-milk cheese was first made in France by Trappist monks. It is a semisoft and very aromatic cheese, similar in flavor to Gouda.

Provolone—An Italian table cheese made from cow's milk. It is eaten fresh or hung and aged, sometimes for as long as a year, and is usually smoked. It can be shaped like a pear, a sausage, or even a pig. It has an ivory-yellow color and a mellow to sharp flavor.

Queso Blanco (white cheese)—The principal cheese of Latin America, queso blanco is made from whole or skimmed cow's milk and is eaten within a few days after it is made. Sometimes the cheese is pressed and then it can be held for 2 weeks or longer.

Ricotta—This Italian cheese, now produced in many other countries, is made from the whey of other cheeses. Fresh, it is very soft and white, with a creamy flavor, and in appearance most nearly resembles cottage cheese. Ricotta cheese is also dried and aged for grating.

Romano (Pecorino Romano)—This very hard Italian sheep's-milk cheese is very popular for grating. Though far cheaper than Parmesan, it should never be substituted for it. Romano is a much stronger and sharper cheese and will upset the balance of flavors in a recipe that calls for Parmesan. Other kinds of Romano are made from cow's or goat's milk.

Roquefort—This great blue-veined sheep's-milk cheese is named after the town of Roquefort-sur-Soulzon in the Aveyron area of France. It has a strong flavor and can be semisoft to hard in texture.

Saint André—An extremely rich cow's-milk cream cheese from France.

Saint-Maure—A French goat's-milk cheese with a strong piquant flavor.

Sapsago—This hard, cow's-milk Swiss or German cheese has powdered clover leaves added to the curd, giving it a pungent flavor and a light green color. Most often used for grating.

Scamorze—An Italian cheese eaten both fresh and aged. It is similar to mozzarella and is made from water buffalo's or cow's milk.

Stilton—Often considered to be the

finest of English cheeses and certainly one of the great cheeses of the world, this blue-veined cow's-milk cheese has a hard but creamy texture. Stilton is probably the mildest of the great blues, but has a rich and piquant flavor.
Selles-sur-Cher—A goat cheese from France's Loire Valley. Mild-tasting but very distinctive.
Swiss—The generic name for the many imitations of Emmental made outside Switzerland. It is a cow's-milk cheese with large holes and a mild, sweet, nutty flavor.
Tilsit—Originally made by Dutch immigrants to East Prussia, this soft but tangy cheese is similar to Havarti.
Valencay—From France. A pyramid-shaped goat cheese with a pronounced flavor.

Buying Cheese

Whenever possible, buy cheese in a compact piece, not a long thin section or slices. The cheese will keep better. If possible, go to a supplier who sells cheese in bulk so you don't have to buy it prepackaged. Always look for high quality. If you are buying cheese for the table, don't make up your mind about what to serve until you get to the cheese store. If the cheese is for cooking, and a cheese in the same family appears to be of better quality, consider whether a substitution is possible. For instance, if you need a Monterey Jack but the Cheddar seems to be better, buy the Cheddar if the dish will not be seriously affected by the change.

It is much easier to inspect cheese if it is free from wrapping, so you can take a close look at its texture and condition. The unwrapped cut surface of a cheese is a good guide to its quality. A hard or semihard cheese such as Cheddar should be firm, even slightly flaky or crumbly, but it should not have cracks in its surface. Nor should it look sweaty or have tiny beads of fat on its surface. These show that the cheese has been kept at too warm a temperature and has been stored for too long. A cheese should be approximately the same color throughout. In general, a darker color near the rind

shows that the cheese is dry and old. White specks or blue sheen indicates mold and a musty flavor. The mold may be scraped away and the cheese used, but the taste will not compare to that of a cheese in prime condition.

Obviously, the best way to decide whether a cheese is of a good quality or has the flavor that you want is to taste it. Even the same type and grade of cheese can vary in flavor and texture. Tasting also helps you to determine the condition of the cheese; for instance, if it has been frozen it may have a flat or oily flavor. A good cheese merchant will usually let you taste before you buy. (In the supermarket, of course, because cheeses are prepackaged, you must rely on the appearance of the cheese and the condition of the packaging.) The milder semisoft cheeses such as Port-Salut and Edam should be velvety when cut, neither moist nor flaky, and should be the same creamy color throughout. They should have a definite cheesy, as opposed to soapy, flavor. A very strong ammoniated odor indicates the cheese is past its prime. On the other hand, the cheese will be tasteless and chalky if underripe. A wedge cut from a whole Brie should be glossy and soft throughout, but should not appear "melted." A Brie will not ripen after it is cut so if there is a hard cakelike white strip through the center, do not buy the cheese. Fresh blue cheeses should be evenly colored without patches of gray; the veins should look crumbly or moist, depending on the type of cheese, and should be widely spaced and stand out in clear-cut contrast to the background color. All blue cheeses are fairly strong and may become harsh as they age, so note the color and texture carefully. Almost all fresh soft cheeses are sold in packages so it is difficult to assess their quality in the store. Look for clean, well-sealed packages that are not discolored or dented.

Some general points to keep in mind when shopping for cheese where cheeses are kept unwrapped, as in a cheese store: Each type of cheese should have its separate place, with space between it and the next type of

cheese. Strong and mild cheeses should not be placed next to each other. Cheeses should be set out on their own rack and should not share space with other strong-flavored foods such as bacon, sausage or ham. Cheese picks up other flavors very easily. Cheeses should look good and well kept. One rusty-looking crust should make you suspect the rest. This kind of damage may indicate poor storage in general.

These days, not only processed but even fancy cheeses come in sealed packages. Since you cannot taste, touch or smell these cheeses, and sometimes cannot even see them, you must note the freshness date stamped on the package. Wrappers should look fresh and clean. Never buy cheese in a torn or a badly dented package. Plastic-wrapped cheeses should be checked closely for tears. There should be no trace of moisture or cloudiness within the package. The shape of the cheese should fill out the package. It should look and feel smooth, not wrinkled or shriveled. Open and examine any packaged cheese as soon as possible. If it is not satisfactory bring it back. Do not keep it in the refrigerator as it may contaminate other foods.

Storing and Serving Cheese

If you have to store cheese, remember that a thin slice is less easy to wrap tightly and does not keep as well. Buy your cheese in chunks—avoid pregrated cheeses—and in fairly small quantities, preferably only enough for one or two meals. Although it does not go bad, cheese tends to lose surface texture and flavor in the refrigerator. The younger cheeses suffer more than the older harder ones, and an opened vacuum-packed cheese may soon grow a mold. Cheese should be kept in the least cold part of the refrigerator, tightly wrapped in aluminum foil. Ideally, hard or semihard cheeses should be used within 2 weeks, semisoft and blue cheeses within 1 week, soft cheeses as soon as possible.

Cheese should not be frozen unless absolutely necessary. Almost any cheese becomes crumbly and grainy in the freezer and will not recover its texture when thawed. It is adequate for cooking but is no longer good as a table cheese. Frozen cheese can be stored for 3 to 4 months.

At least 1 hour before serving, remove the cheese from the refrigerator; unwrap and let stand at room temperature to allow the flavor of the cheese to develop.

Cheese at the Table. Almost any cheese is delicious served as it is and for many people a wedge of cheese is an essential part of a meal or a party. For a regular meal it is easier to serve just one kind of cheese, but for a larger dinner or for a party, several cheeses are in order. When putting together a cheese selection, keep in mind the different types of cheese and try to represent them well. You may want to serve one hard or semihard cheese, one soft creamy cheese, and one blue-veined cheese. For a cocktail party you may choose several from each category. Or, for a dinner or a cocktail party, you may prefer to serve several different varieties in the same category—a beautiful selection of *chèvres*, for example.

Cheese is best served on a wooden board, rather than a glass or ceramic surface, which will blunt the edge of a cheese knife. If possible each cheese should have its own knife, slicer or spoon so that the flavors will not be mixed. For hard and semihard cheese, the proper knife is one with a pronged end, which permits you to pick up the cheese after you have sliced it. Semisoft cheeses are best cut into thin slices with a cheese slicer, which is pulled across the cheese. Very soft cheeses are often served with a spoon.

Most people tend to eat cheese with crackers, bread or fruit, but because there are some people who like to eat cheese with a knife and fork, silver should be laid out when serving cheese at a party.

Setting Up a Cheeseboard. Present the cheeses well. Buy neat portions of about the same size. Lay them out, spaced well apart, each with its own knife. If the cheese is your dessert course, decorate the tray with several varieties of grapes, slices of apple and pear that have been dipped in lemon juice to prevent browning, segments of oranges, and other fruit. Serve the bread, crackers and butter separately.

HOMEMADE CHEESES

Simple curd and cream cheeses can be made at home with a minimum of special equipment. Some of the cheeses can be made without the use of special cheese starters.

Equipment

Thermometer—You should use a thermometer to insure that the milk is at the proper temperature. Using milk that is at the wrong temperature is one of the primary reasons homemade cheese fails. A dairy thermometer is best but an accurate candy thermometer will work for the basic cheese recipes given here.

Measuring cup—A large measuring cup is necessary to insure that the milk is measured accurately.

Mixing bowls—Several large mixing bowls are needed to hold the milk and the cheese at the various stages of preparation. Do not use plastic bowls as they can harbor bacteria.

Cheesecloth—Cheesecloth is needed for draining the whey from the curd. You can also use very fine muslin or a clean dish towel.

Colander—A colander is needed to support the cheesecloth while you spoon in the curd.

Molds—Soft cheeses were traditionally made in their own distinctively shaped molds. You can improvise with anything from a terra cotta flowerpot to a can into which you have punched drainage holes. Whatever you choose, it must be sterilized. Pretty heart-shaped or round pottery molds can be found in kitchen specialty shops.

Ingredients

Milk—All cheese is made from milk, whether it is from the cow, goat, ewe, or water buffalo. Milk has two characteristics that are important in cheese making. One is the ability of liquid milk to clot and become a solid curd, and the other is milk's ability to sour and become more acidic.

Milk clots because it contains a protein called casein, which separates into a solid when rennet is added or when the milk sours and becomes very high in acid. Milk turns sour because of the presence of lactose or milk sugar. Lactose is changed to lactic acid by bacteria naturally present in untreated milk. These bacteria will cause souring when the milk is kept in warm conditions for an extended time. Pasteurized milk, however, does not have a sufficient number of these bacteria to sour the milk properly on its own; that is, to sour it in a way that is suitable for cheese making. Therefore it is necessary to add something to the milk to make it clot and sour. This is usually called cheese starter. Treated long-life milks are not suitable for cheese making.

Cream—Heavy cream is used in many cheese recipes.

Rennet—Rennet is a substance that is found in the stomachs of very young animals; when they nurse, the rennet clots the milk, making it easier to digest. Rennet works best when the milk has already begun to sour. Rennet tablets used in making desserts are sometimes available from grocers and can be used to make certain soft cheeses. It is also available in liquid form at health food stores. Special cheese rennet, available from cheese-making suppliers, gives better results. The amount of dessert rennet varies from recipe to recipe. If using cheese rennet or liquid rennet, follow the manufacturer's instructions.

Salt—Salt helps to preserve cheese and to bring out its flavor.

10

Cheese starter—Cheese starter is milk containing a special bacterial culture. It is responsible for producing the necessary level of acidity during cheese making and it contributes to the flavor of the cheese. Not all cheeses require a special starter; some can be made with rennet alone.* Other homemade cheeses, known as acid curd cheeses, are made by simply adding lemon juice to the milk.

Flavorings

After making homemade cheese, you may flavor it in any way that you wish. The flavored cheese should be eaten within a day or two of preparation.

Herbs—Snipped fresh chives, sage, basil and parsley are delicious in fresh cheese. Chop the desired herbs fine and stir into the cheese until it is flecked with green throughout.

Garlic—Garlic can be used in combination with herbs or alone. Use fresh garlic put through a press or pounded to a paste in a mortar and add it to taste. Do not use garlic powder or garlic salt.

Nuts—Nuts can be chopped and added to the cheese or small balls of fresh cheese may be rolled in them. Toasting raw nuts first will give them additional flavor. Place them on a baking sheet and set in a 350°F oven for a few minutes, or until lightly browned.

Fruit—Fresh or dried fruit can be chopped and stirred into the cheese, or you can sweeten the cheese and serve with the fruit. Fruit is an especially good addition to fresh cream cheese.

Seafood—Finely chopped anchovies, shrimps, or crab meat make a tasty addition to a spreadable cheese. Add enough to flavor but not overpower the cheese.

Vegetables—Finely chopped cooked mushrooms, red or green pepper, cucumber, celery or scallions make good additions to a spreadable cheese.

*Cheese starter and rennet are available by mail from the New England Cheesemaking Supply Company, Box 85, Main Street, Ashfield, Massachusetts 01330, and the Erie Cheesemaking Supply Company, 7700 West Bargain Road, Erie, Pennsylvania 16509.

Making Fresh Soft Cheese

makes 8 to 10 ounces

1 quart pasteurized milk or goat's milk
1 dessert rennet tablet
salt

1 Heat the milk in a heavy saucepan or double boiler and set over low heat until it reaches 100°F on a dairy or candy thermometer.

4 Line a colander with a double thickness of cheesecloth. Uncover the bowl of cheese curds.

5 Using a slotted spoon or stainless knife, scoop out a piece of the curd. Place it in the colander, allowing the whey to drip through.

8 Transfer the bag of cheese to a mold or other container that has drainage holes at the base.

9 Place the mold on a board or rack suspended over a large bowl or pan to catch dripping whey. Leave for 4 to 5 hours.

2 Dissolve the rennet tablet in 2 tablespoons cold water. Transfer the milk to a large bowl.

3 Stir the rennet into the milk. Cover with a clean cloth. Let set in a warm place for 2 hours, or until curd has set.

6 Gradually add all the curd. Add salt to taste. Gather up the ends of the cheesecloth and tie into a bag, using heavy string.

7 Hang bag from hook. Place bowl underneath bag to catch whey. Allow cheese to drip for about 2 hours. At least once, open bag and move curd around.

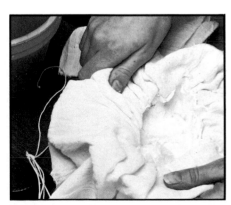

10 Untie the bag of cheese, gently easing away the cheesecloth. To keep the cheese in the shape of mold, invert it onto a plate.

11 If you wish to flavor the cheese, scrape the cheese into a bowl and add desired flavorings.

Making Cheese

Making cheese at home is very easy. Begin with the simple Fresh Soft Cheese, illustrated here, to familiarize yourself with basic cheese-making steps.

Heating the milk—Milk must be heated, but not boiled, to activate the rennet or the cheese starter. The recipe will specify the proper temperature. Heat the milk in a heavy saucepan or a double boiler, so that the milk will not scorch, then check the temperature with a candy or a dairy thermometer.

Dissolving the rennet—The rennet tablet should be placed in just enough water to dissolve it. For dessert rennet, use approximately 2 tablespoons of cold water to 1 tablet. Follow the manufacturer's instructions for liquid rennet and cheese rennet.

Adding the milk—The milk should be transferred to a large bowl; then the dissolved rennet tablet should be stirred in until it is thoroughly combined with the milk. Then add the salt and stir well. Cover the milk with a clean cloth and leave it undisturbed in a warm place for about 2 hours. This is called the incubation period. At the end of this time the rennet should have coagulated the milk.

Draining—Just before the end of the incubation period, line a colander with a double thickness of washed cheesecloth or a clean dish towel. Using a slotted spoon or stainless steel knife, slice off a little of the set milk curd, and place it in the lined colander. The liquid whey will run off. As the whey runs out of the colander and the curd settles, add more curd, repeating until all the curd is added to the colander. Then gather the top of the cloth together and tie securely with string. Suspend the cloth from a hook in a cool, well-ventilated room, positioning a bowl underneath to catch the dripping whey. Allow the cheese to drain this way for about 2 hours. To encourage even drainage, open the bag at least once and move the curd so that the area that was on the outside is moved to the center.

Molding the cheese—After hanging,

the cheese is ready to be molded. Place the bag of cheese in a clean, sterilized mold with a drainage hole at the base. A flowerpot is perfect. Place the mold on a rack or board that is suspended over a bowl to catch the remaining whey. Leave the cheese in the mold for 4 to 5 hours.

Unmolding the cheese—Untie the string on the cheesecloth and gently peel the cloth back from the top of the cheese. Place an inverted plate on top of the mold and, holding the two together, invert them. Remove the mold and gently remove the cheese-cloth. Serve the cheese in its molded shape or break it up and flavor the cheese as desired. To store, wrap the cheese well and place in the refrigera-tor for up to 3 days.

Using the whey—The whey can be used in baking. It is especially good in muffins and scones, used as part of the liquid. Or do as Little Miss Muffet did and make a dish of curds and whey. Break up the cheese slightly and pour the whey over it. Add some fresh cream, sprinkle with sugar, and eat plain or with fruit.

HOMEMADE YOGURT

Yogurt has enjoyed a popularity boom in recent years—not surprising when you consider what a tasty and nutritious food it is. Fruit-flavored or plain, it makes a great snack or break-fast or light lunch. Plain, it is used in main dishes and salads from many parts of the world, and makes a deli-cious, less caloric substitute for sour cream. By making your own yogurt, you can have an endless and economi-cal supply, with a flavor and con-sistency tailored to your taste and freshness you could never find on the supermarket shelf.

Making Yogurt

makes about 2 cups

1 pint pasteurized homogenized milk
or 1 pint pasteurized homogenized milk plus 4 ounces dried skimmed milk powder
or 4 ounces dried skimmed milk powder plus boiling water
or 1 cup evaporated milk plus boiling water
2 tablespoons unpasteurized plain yogurt

1 For a thin yogurt, boil pasteur-ized milk for 5 minutes. For thicker yogurt, boil the milk until it has reduced to two thirds of its original volume.

3 If using blanket method, warm the blanket. Rinse out the bowl with hot water and dry. If using a Thermos, rinse out with hot water.

4 When the milk has reached 115°F, stir a little into the starter. Then whisk mixture into the remaining milk. Transfer mixture to bowl or Thermos.

What is yogurt? Milk, simply milk. It contains almost all the goodness of the milk that you use to make it and very little else. So why doesn't it have the consistency and flavor of plain milk? Why does it have a pudding tex-ture and a slightly sharper taste? The answer comes from those microor-ganisms that we call bacteria. Not all bacteria are friendly, but there are three friendly types that are essential in mak-ing yogurt. When these living bacilli are added to milk that has been heated to the right temperature, they feed and breed. As they feed, they make the milk more acid so that the solid milk parti-cles stick together, producing a soft custard-like mass. All yogurt, unless it has been pasteurized or has gone bad, has live cultures in it.

When you buy commercial yo-gurt, not only are you paying more for it than homemade, but you are getting an often bland, standardized product. The only clue to its age is the date stamped on the container. When you

OR If using pasteurized homogenized milk plus powder, boil the milk for 15 minutes, then mix in the powder.

OR If using powder alone, mix with 1 pint of just-boiled water. If using evaporated milk, mix with an equal volume of just-boiled water. For thicker yogurt, reduce mixture as in step 1.

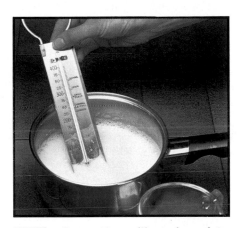

2 Cover the milk and cool to 115°F. Place the starter in a bowl or measuring cup.

5 Place bowl in turned-off oven with pilot light. Or wrap bowl in plastic wrap, blanket, and plastic—or seal Thermos. Transfer to incubating place.

6 Let stand for 3 to 5 hours. When curd has formed, cool bowl to room temperature. Cool Thermos in cold water for 5 minutes.

7 Transfer yogurt in Thermos to a bowl. Refrigerate yogurt for at least 1 hour before using.

make your own yogurt, it is always fresh and the thickness and flavor can be varied to suit your taste or the requirements of a particular dish (for instance, a mild thick yogurt will not give the same results as a thinner acidic one).

Essential Ingredients

The two essential ingredients for yogurt making are starter and milk. Starter—Dried starter, containing live, healthy, yogurt-producing bacilli, can be purchased from health food stores or from manufacturers of electric yogurt makers. However, unflavored, unpasteurized commercial yogurt can be used equally well. About 1½ tablespoons of commercial yogurt is sufficient to turn about 1 pint of milk into yogurt. Once you have made your first batch you can store some of it as starter for your next batch. Do this with each successive batch until you have repeated the process about 20 times; after that the yogurt will be too thin and you will need a new starter.

Milk—You can use various forms of milk, alone or mixed. Some make thicker yogurt than others (see below), so choose your milk according to the style of yogurt you prefer.

Equipment

Measuring cup and a set of measuring spoons—To measure milk and starter. Funnel—Useful, particularly if you are making starter. 1-quart bowl—For mixing the yogurt.

Wire whisk—To blend the starter. Thermometer—Useful for determining the temperature of the milk.

Incubation

An incubator is used to keep the yogurt warm until it is ready. A covered bowl, wrapped in a warm blanket, is simple and it works. (Wrap the bowl and blanket in plastic to keep the heat in.) A wide-mouth Thermos jug can be used for the same purpose and is easier to manage. Perhaps easiest of all is to place the yogurt in a bowl and set it in a closed, turned-off oven with a pilot light. An electric yogurt maker is handy, but the quality of the yogurt made this way is perhaps not quite as high as that made by other methods.

Making the Yogurt

This method of making yogurt can be used with the blanket method, the Thermos method, and the oven method. If you have an electric yogurt maker, follow the manufacturer's instructions.

Preparing the milk—Choose the milk you want to use and bring it to a boil.

Fresh raw cow's or goat's milk— Boil the milk for about 15 minutes or until it has reduced to two thirds of its original volume. For a thinner yogurt, boil for 5 minutes only. Cool milk to 115°F before adding starter.

Pasteurized homogenized milk— Process as for raw milk.

Pasteurized homogenized milk mixed with dried milk powder—Boil the milk down for 15 minutes, or until it is reduced by two thirds, and then mix in 2 to 4 ounces of dried milk powder to every pint of milk. This produces a very thick creamy yogurt, like the ones eaten in Greece. Cool milk to 115°F before adding starter.

Dried skimmed milk powder— Use 1 pint of boiling water to each 4 ounces of powder to produce a thick yogurt. Then add starter.

Unsweetened canned evaporated milk—Use one part milk to one part boiling water (plus starter) to make a custardy yogurt, or three quarters part boiling water to one part milk to make an even thicker yogurt.

For all of these, the amount of liquid you start with is the amount of yogurt you should end up with.

After boiling, remove milk from the heat and cover it to prevent a skin from forming. Let the milk cool to 115°F before using. It is important to have the milk at the right temperature, so use a thermometer for your first few batches.

Preparing for incubation—You will need a place where the yogurt can stand at a constant temperature of 100°F for several hours. To keep the container of yogurt at this temperature, the surrounding temperature should be about 115°F. An oven with a pilot light, a warm cupboard, the top of a radiator, or any other warm place that comes to mind, should suffice as the incubator.

While the milk is cooling, get the equipment ready. If you are using the blanket method, set the blanket over a radiator to warm, if possible. If you are using a Thermos, rinse it out with boiling water so that it is hot when the yogurt mixture is poured in. If you are using a bowl, rinse the bowl with hot water and dry.

Adding the starter—Place the starter in a measuring cup or bowl. Pour in a little of the warm milk and mix. Pour this mixture back into the milk and whisk until just blended. Transfer the milk to the bowl or Thermos. If using the bowl and blanket method, cover with plastic wrap, then wrap in the blanket, then in additional plastic. If using the oven method, leave bowl as is.

Incubating—Transfer the yogurt to the incubating place, cover and let sit undisturbed for 3 hours. Check to see if a curd has formed. If not, let incubate for another hour or two. Do not let the yogurt incubate past the point at which it has set and acquired a custardy texture, or it will become too sour. Remove it from the blanket, the Thermos or the oven and let the yogurt cool to room temperature. Transfer to the refrigerator to chill for at least an hour. If using a Thermos, cool to room temperature by standing the Thermos in a bowl of cold water for 5 minutes.

Thickening the yogurt—Now that you have made the yogurt, there are several ways to thicken it further, if desired. (Before you proceed, set aside and refrigerate several tablespoons of the yogurt to use as starter for your next batch of yogurt.)

Thickening Yogurt

1 For very thick yogurt, line a sieve with dampened cheesecloth. Place over a bowl.

2 Spoon the yogurt into the sieve and allow to drip for 3 hours. For even thicker curdlike yogurt, let drip for 6 hours.

If you want a very thick cheeselike yogurt, you must drain some of the liquid from the yogurt. To do this, line a sieve with a double thickness of dampened cheesecloth and place the sieve over a bowl. Spoon the yogurt into the lined sieve and let the whey drip through for about 3 hours. As in cheese making, this whey can be used for baking.

In India and parts of the Middle East, an even thicker yogurt, almost like cottage cheese, is used in many dishes. To make this yogurt, let the yogurt drip in the sieve for an additional 5 to 6 hours. This thicker yogurt is particularly suited to cooking.

Storing the Yogurt

Yogurt will keep in the refrigerator for about a week, remaining fairly mild for a few days and then becoming noticeably thicker and sharper-tasting.

Flavoring Yogurt

There are several ways to flavor yogurt. You can infuse it with strongly flavored solid ingredients that will be removed before serving; you can stir powdered or liquid flavoring into the yogurt; or you can add solids that will remain to be eaten with the yogurt. Whichever kind of flavoring you choose, add it after the yogurt incubates so that the flavoring will not interfere with the work of the yogurt-making bacilli. Although stirring the yogurt will break up the curd, it will thicken again after chilling, so you may want to add any flavorings to remain in the yogurt an hour or two before serving. Likewise, this is the best time to remove any solids that are being used just for flavoring.

Infused flavors—These flavorings disturb the yogurt's texture least. You can add some, a bay leaf for example, leaving part of it above the yogurt's surface for easy removal. If ingredients lend themselves to it, skewer them before adding for easy removal. Any or several of the following work well:

  bay leaf
  slice of onion
  garlic clove
  scallion
  chunk of horseradish
  sprig of either mint, dill, thyme, tarragon, rosemary, basil or sage
  cinnamon stick

Stirred-in flavors—Powdered or liquid ingredients are usually mixed in so that the flavor is distributed evenly. Yogurt flavored this way can be eaten alone or used as a topping for another dish. Add the following flavorings to taste:

  salt
  pepper: white, black or cayenne
  ground spices: cinnamon, nutmeg, allspice or ginger
  curry powder
  sesame seeds
  crushed or ground herbs: dill, fennel, thyme, mint, marjoram, sage or coriander
  Worcestershire sauce
  vinegar: wine, cider or fruit or herb-flavored ones
  anchovy paste
  ketchup: tomato, mushroom, walnut
  chutney: mango or any other fruit flavor
  sugar: granulated, brown or confectioners'
  grated orange, lemon or lime rind
  liqueur
  fruit purée
  honey, molasses, maple syrup
  vanilla, lemon or almond extract

Solid additions—This group is the most versatile since so many ingredients go well with yogurt. They can be placed on the surface of the yogurt or stirred in. If the ingredient contains excess liquid, blot before adding, so as not to thin the yogurt. The ingredients should be chopped fine, shredded, or grated:

  pickles
  olives: green or black
  bell peppers: red, green, yellow
  carrot
  cucumber
  onion
  dillweed
  bulb fennel
  smoked fish: trout, salmon, bluefish, oysters
  canned fish: herring, mackerel, sardines, anchovy fillets
  shrimp or other shellfish
  ham or other smoked meat or poultry
  hard-cooked eggs
  cheese
  fruit: canned, candied, dried or fresh (if using fresh, add shortly before serving or the fruit will become soggy)
  nuts
  chocolate
  dried coconut
  candy: peppermints, fudge, nut brittle
  cookies or meringues

Some other ideas:

Yogurt makes a tasty salad when mixed with chopped bell peppers, scallions, apple and walnuts or peanuts.

Mix thickened yogurt with egg yolk, chives and a dash of Tabasco® to make a filling for hard-cooked eggs or tomatoes.

Use yogurt instead of mayonnaise for a tangy flavor and a less caloric dressing. Mix with a spoonful of ketchup for a shrimp cocktail sauce, a dash of mustard for poultry.

For a refreshing appetizer, mix about 1 part very thick yogurt to 2 parts cream cheese. Season to taste and roll in walnuts.

Mix yogurt and chives to make a dressing for baked potatoes.

For an unusual and tasty salad dressing, combine yogurt, crumbled bacon, a dash of lemon juice and a good grinding of black pepper.

Flavored yogurt is excellent over hot vegetables.

Use yogurt as a replacement for sour cream to give good flavor with less calories.

Replace half the whipped cream in dessert fillings, mousses and cold puddings with a thick yogurt.

Flavor yogurt with honey and add crushed berries. Transfer to a bowl and top with a layer of graham cracker crumbs.

Combine yogurt with granola, substituting it for milk.

Stir melted semisweet chocolate into yogurt to make instant chocolate pudding with a little something extra.

Blue Cheese Log

This log can be made in advance and refrigerated until needed. Cut into slices and serve with water biscuits or other crackers.

makes about thirty ¼-inch-thick slices

4 ounces (½ cup) cottage cheese	1 tablespoon snipped fresh chives
4 ounces Danish or other crumbly blue cheese, at room temperature	2 ounces black olives
	1 tablespoon brandy
	2 ounces whole salted peanuts

Press the cottage cheese through a sieve into a bowl. Add blue cheese and blend cheeses with a fork until creamy. Stir in the chives. Pit the olives and chop fine. Add to the cheese along with the brandy; mix until blended.

Wet your hands and shape the cheese mixture into a log about 1 inch across. Roll in the peanuts. Cover and refrigerate for at least 1 hour before serving.

English Potted Cheese

Potting cheese is an old English custom and a good way to make a small amount of cheese go a long way for a party. This can be made 3 or 4 days ahead.

makes about 2 cups

1 pound Cheshire, Double Gloucester, or sharp Cheddar cheese, at room temperature	6 tablespoons unsalted butter, at room temperature
pinch of cayenne pepper	¼ teaspoon ground mace
	pinch of dry mustard
	½ cup sweet sherry

Grate the cheese into a medium-size bowl. Add the pepper, butter, mace and mustard; beat until smooth. Stir in the sherry. The mixture should have the consistency of a mousse. Spoon the mixture into a small earthenware crock and smooth the top. Cover and refrigerate for at least 1 day to allow the flavors to mellow. Serve with crackers.

Blue Cheese Dip

This dip is delicious with fresh crusty bread or crisp celery sticks.

makes about 1 cup

4   ounces Danish or other crumbly blue cheese, at room temperature

3   ounces cream cheese, at room temperature
1   tablespoon lemon juice pinch of salt

Beat the blue cheese and cream cheese together in a small bowl. Add the lemon juice and salt and stir to make a smooth cream. Cover and refrigerate for at least 30 minutes before serving.

Roquefort Dressing

Serve this delicious dressing with a green salad or a bowl of plain cold boiled shrimp.

makes about 1 cup

1   cup Vinaigrette Dressing (see Volume 1 Index)
2   ounces Roquefort cheese

1   tablespoon snipped fresh chives

Place the dressing in a small bowl. Add the cheese and mash until the mixture is well blended. Stir in the chives. Serve immediately or store in the refrigerator, covered, for up to 1 hour.

Potted Stilton

This delicious spiced and potted cheese spread is an excellent way to use up Stilton or any other blue cheese past its prime. It is good on crackers or crusty bread, but it is particularly tasty when used to sandwich walnut halves together. It will keep in the refrigerator for about 3 weeks.

makes about 2 cups

1 pound Stilton or other blue cheese, at room temperature	salt
	ground mace
	1 tablespoon port or Madeira
8 tablespoons unsalted butter, at room temperature	4 tablespoons Clarified Butter (see Volume 3 Index)

Cut any rind from the cheese and crumble the cheese into a bowl, discarding any hard dark lumps. Add the butter, and cream together with the cheese until smooth. Season with salt and mace to taste. Add the port, a few drops at a time, working the mixture to a smooth paste. Spoon the mixture into small earthenware pots, or 1 large one, leaving at least

½ inch headspace. Tap the crock two or three times on the counter to knock out any air pockets. Smooth the top of the mixture. Melt the clarified butter; pour enough over the potted Stilton to make a thin layer. When solidified, pour over another layer. Cover the pots and refrigerate for at least 1 day, or as long as 3 weeks.

Roquefort and Brandy Spread

This sophisticated spread is delicious with Melba toast. If stored in an airtight container, it will keep in the refrigerator for up to 2 weeks.

makes about 1¼ cups

8 ounces Roquefort cheese, at room temperature

4 tablespoons unsalted butter, at room temperature

¼ teaspoon grated nutmeg

¼ cup brandy

Crumble the Roquefort into a small bowl. Add the butter and beat until the mixture is smooth. Stir in the nutmeg and brandy and beat until the ingredients are well blended. Spoon the mixture into a small serving bowl or individual ramekins. Serve immediately or refrigerate until 30 minutes before serving and then let stand at room temperature to soften.

Marinated Goat Cheese

4 to 6 portions

8 to 12 ounces fresh goat cheese, such as Montrachet

½ cup small Niçoise olives

½ teaspoon whole black peppercorns

1 garlic clove

2 to 3 sprigs of fresh herbs (thyme, oregano, or marjoram), or 1½ teaspoons dried

1 small bay leaf good-quality olive oil

Cut the cheese into ¾-inch slices and place it in a serving bowl. Add the olives. Wrap the peppercorns in the end of a towel and crush with the back of a cleaver or a heavy pot. Add to cheese. Peel the garlic and cut into quarters. Add to the cheese along with the herbs and bay leaf. Pour over just enough olive oil to cover the cheese. Let ingredients marinate at room temperature for several hours or make a day ahead, refrigerate, and bring to room temperature before serving. Serve with crusty bread.

Variation: Before adding olive oil, add ¼ cup slivered sun-dried tomatoes. The tomatoes are expensive but add unique flavor to this dish.

Herbed Goat Cheese Spread

This can be made with cream cheese, if you prefer, though the goat cheese gives it a nice tang.

makes about 1 cup

8 ounces fresh creamy goat cheese, such as Montrachet

1 garlic clove

1 tablespoon chopped fresh parsley

pinch of dried thyme or leaves from a sprig of fresh thyme

salt and freshly ground pepper

In a medium-size bowl, beat the cheese until smooth. Put the garlic clove through a press and add to the cheese along with the parsley and thyme. Beat until well blended. Season to taste with salt and pepper. Cover and refrigerate for at least 1 hour, to allow flavors to mellow. Leave at room temperature for 20 minutes before serving and accompany with crackers or crusty bread.

Creamy Cheese

This easy-to-make creamy cheese requires no special equipment. Sprinkled with a bit of sugar and served with fruit, it makes a delicious dessert, or, with a few chopped chives, a tasty sandwich spread.

makes about 2 cups

1¼ cups heavy cream	⅛ teaspoon salt
⅔ cup milk	

Set a medium-size bowl in a larger pan or bowl half-full of ice cubes. Pour the cream and milk into the smaller bowl. Let mixture sit in the ice bath for 30 minutes to chill thoroughly.

Add the salt. Using a wire whisk or rotary beater, whip the cream and milk mixture until it is thick and creamy but not stiff. Cut a piece of cheesecloth large enough to line a colander, and immerse the cloth in boiling water. Rinse the cheesecloth in cold water, wring it out, and use it to line the colander. Set the colander over a bowl. Spoon the cream mixture into the colander. Cover lightly and refrigerate for about 12 hours, or until the cheese has drained completely and is firm.

Invert the cheese onto a serving dish. Remove the colander and the cheesecloth and serve the cheese.

Normandy Cheese Spread

This rich creamy spread is excellent on thin slices of black bread. If Calvados is unavailable, applejack or Cognac can be substituted.

makes about 1 cup

3 ounces Roquefort cheese, at room temperature	⅛ teaspoon freshly ground pepper
3 ounces cream cheese, at room temperature	¼ teaspoon grated nutmeg
2 tablespoons butter, at room temperature	2 tablespoons Calvados
	2 tablespoons chopped pickled walnuts*

Crumble the Roquefort cheese into a small bowl. Add the cream cheese and butter and beat until smooth and creamy. Beat in the pepper, nutmeg and Calvados. Stir in the pickled walnuts. Serve at once or store, covered, in the refrigerator for up to 3 days. If refrigerated, let stand at room temperature for 30 minutes before serving.

*Pickled walnuts are generally available in specialty food stores.

Rich Cream Cheese

This is a delicious homemade cheese. Although it is not necessary, cheese starter can be added to improve the storage quality of the cheese. If you decide to use starter, add ½ teaspoon after the cream has been heated. This cheese can be used in any recipe calling for cream cheese.

makes 5 to 6 ounces

1 pint heavy cream	1 dessert rennet tablet
1½ teaspoons salt	

Place the cream in a double boiler or in a bowl placed over a pan of simmering water. Heat the cream to 75°F. Remove from heat. Stir in the salt. Cover the cream and leave in a warm place for 2 to 3 hours.

Dissolve rennet in 2 tablespoons cold water. Stir into the cream; cover again and leave in a warm place for 12 hours.

Line a colander with a double thickness of cheesecloth. Ladle the coagulated cream into it a little at a time, letting it drain after each addition. Gather up the cheesecloth and tie securely with string. Hang the bag from a hook in a cool well-ventilated room and let drain over a bowl for about 12 hours. To insure even drainage, open the bag several times during the dripping, and move the curd so the area that was on the outside is moved to the center and vice versa. When sufficiently drained the cheese will be thick and appear granular. Store in the refrigerator for up to 3 days.

Roquefort and Cream Cheese Ring

*This ring, garnished with olives and tomatoes, makes a
tasty and colorful centerpiece for a buffet table.*

makes a 1-quart ring,
about 8 portions

2	teaspoons vegetable oil
2	envelopes (2 scant tablespoons) unflavored gelatin
¼	cup water
6	ounces Roquefort cheese, at room temperature
8	ounces cream cheese, at room temperature
¼	teaspoon cayenne pepper
1	teaspoon anchovy paste
2	scallions
¾	cup Mayonnaise (see Volume 3 Index)
¾	cup heavy cream
2	medium-size tomatoes
8	stuffed green olives
8	lettuce leaves

Coat a 1-quart ring mold with the vegetable oil. Place the ring upside down on a sheet of paper toweling to drain off excess oil.

Place the cold water in a small saucepan; sprinkle the gelatin over the water and let stand 2 minutes. Heat the gelatin over very low heat until it liquefies. Set aside to cool slightly.

Crumble the Roquefort into a fine sieve. Place the sieve over a medium-size mixing bowl and, with the back of a wooden spoon, press the cheese through it. Add the cream cheese, cayenne and anchovy paste and beat until well blended. Trim the scallions and, reserving the white for another use, chop the green to measure 2 tablespoons. Beat into the cheese.

Quickly stir the dissolved gelatin into the cheese mixture and continue stirring until well blended. With a spatula or large spoon, fold the mayonnaise and the heavy cream into the cheese mixture. Pour the cheese mixture into the oiled mold. Cover and refrigerate until the mold has set, at least 1 hour.

At serving time, remove the ring mold from the refrigerator and quickly dip the bottom into hot water. Place a serving plate over the mold and invert. Lift off the mold; the ring should slide out easily. Slice the tomatoes and halve the olives. Garnish the ring with the tomato slices, olives and lettuce leaves.

Uppingham Pâté

This is a creamy, sharp-flavored pâté, adapted from an old English recipe. It is delicious served as a first course or cheese course along with hot toast, or as a dessert, accompanied by fruit.

makes about 4 cups, 8 to 10 portions

1	large onion
1	large carrot
2	celery ribs
	bouquet garni: 4 parsley sprigs, 1 thyme sprig, 1 bay leaf
3	cups milk
6	tablespoons butter
¾	cup all-purpose flour

3	tablespoons Mayonnaise (see Volume 3 Index)
2	teaspoons lemon juice
3	garlic cloves
10	stuffed green olives
½	teaspoon salt
½	teaspoon freshly ground black pepper
⅛	teaspoon cayenne pepper
12	ounces Stilton cheese

Peel the onion and chop it into coarse pieces. Peel the carrot and chop it. Trim the celery and chop it. Place the vegetables in a medium-size saucepan. Prepare the *bouquet garni,* tying the ingredients together in cheesecloth, and add to the saucepan along with the milk. Heat to boiling over medium-high heat, then reduce heat and simmer, covered, for 15 minutes. Remove the pan from the heat and set aside until milk has cooled to room temperature. When cool, pour the milk through a fine-mesh sieve into a large mixing bowl. Press the vegetables to extract any juices. Discard the contents of the sieve and set the milk aside.

Rinse and dry the saucepan, add the butter and melt over medium heat. When the foam subsides, remove the saucepan from the heat and stir in the flour with a wooden spoon, blending to make a smooth paste. Gradually add the milk, stirring constantly. Return the pan to medium heat and cook, still stirring constantly, for 2 to 3 minutes, or until the sauce is very thick and smooth. Remove the pan from heat and set sauce aside to cool to room temperature.

When the sauce is cool, beat in the mayonnaise and lemon juice, peel the garlic, press it, and add it to the sauce. Chop the olives fine and add to the sauce along with the salt, pepper and cayenne. Cut the rind from the Stilton and crumble the cheese into a fine-mesh sieve set over a medium-size bowl. Using the back of a wooden spoon, press the cheese through the sieve. Beat the cheese into the sauce until the mixture is smooth and the ingredients are thoroughly combined. Spoon the mixture into a serving bowl. Smooth the surface with the back of the spoon. Cover and refrigerate for 1 hour, or until pâté is chilled and set. Remove the pâté from the refrigerator and serve immediately.

Cottage Cheese

This low-fat cottage cheese can also be made with reconstituted skimmed milk powder.

makes about 8 ounces

1   pint skimmed milk
2   tablespoons cheese starter

1   dessert rennet tablet

In a heavy saucepan, heat the milk to 90°F. Pour into a bowl; add the cheese starter and stir well. Dissolve the rennet tablet in 2 tablespoons of cold water; stir into the cheese mixture. Cover and leave in a warm place for 2 hours.

Cut the curd into 1-inch cubes with a stainless steel knife. The easiest way to do this is to invert the curd onto a clean plate and cut first horizontally, then vertically. Place the cubes in the top of a double boiler and set over simmering water. Heat to 90°F, stirring constantly. Remove from the heat and let stand, covered, for 10 minutes.

Line a colander with a double thickness of cheesecloth and spoon some of the curds into it. Let drain and add more curd, a spoonful at a time. Gather up the cheesecloth and tie securely with string. Hang from a hook in a cool well-ventilated room and let drain over a bowl for 4 hours. To insure even drainage, open bag several times to move curd so that the area that was on the outside is moved to the center and vice versa. Change cheesecloth once. Remove the cheese from the cheesecloth; transfer to a bowl and season to taste. Refrigerate for up to 3 days.

Variation: For rich cottage cheese, stir 3 tablespoons light cream into the curds before refrigerating.

Tvorog

(Russian Buttermilk Cottage Cheese)

Russians love cottage cheese as much as their American counterparts and often make their own at home. You will be tempted to do the same when you discover just how easy this method is, and the cheese is tangy and extremely low in calories.

makes about 2 cups

2   quarts cultured buttermilk in cartons

Place the sealed cartons of buttermilk in a deep pot (at least 8 inches high) and fill the pot with water, leaving 2 inches of space at the top. Bring the water to a boil and lower the heat so that the water simmers. Simmer for 15 minutes. Remove the pot from the heat and allow the buttermilk to cool completely in the water bath. Leave the containers overnight if you wish. Line a colander or sieve with several layers of cheesecloth and pour the contents of the buttermilk cartons into the cheesecloth. The whey will have separated from the curds while in the cartons, but you should let the cheese drain for about 1 hour. If you like a drier cottage cheese, tie the cheesecloth into a tight sack and allow to drain longer. Remove to a plastic container and refrigerate.

Lemon Cheese

This acid curd cheese, made simply with lemon juice and cow's or goat's milk, is moist and easy to spread. It is tasty eaten plain, but can also be sweetened and served with fruit or made savory by the addition of herbs.

makes 4 to 5 ounces

1   pint milk
1   lemon

salt

Heat the milk in a heavy saucepan to 100°F. Transfer the milk to a bowl. Squeeze the juice from the lemon and strain it into the milk, stirring to blend. Cover and leave in a warm place for 15 minutes.

Line a colander with a double thickness of cheesecloth. When the milk has set, ladle the curd in, a little at a time, allowing the whey to drip through before you add more. Gather up the cheesecloth and tie securely with string. Hang over a bowl and let drip in a cool well-ventilated room for 1 hour. Untie the cheesecloth and scoop the cheese into a bowl. Season or flavor to taste.

Liptauer Käse

(Hungarian Cheese Spread)

You can make this popular spread at home for a fraction of the delicatessen price. Very well covered, the cheese may be stored in the refrigerator for up to 1 week.

makes about 8 ounces

4	ounces (½ cup) cottage cheese, homemade or commercial	½	teaspoon caraway seeds
8	tablespoons unsalted butter, at room temperature	1	teaspoon Dijon-style mustard
		¼	teaspoon salt
		1½	teaspoons paprika
1	tablespoon anchovy paste		capers
2	teaspoons minced gherkins		radishes
			black olives

Cream the butter. Add the cottage cheese and beat with butter until soft and blended. One at a time, add anchovy paste, gherkins, caraway seeds, Dijon-style mustard, salt and paprika, beating well after each addition.

Spoon the cheese onto a serving plate and refrigerate for 5 minutes. Shape into a cylinder, using a long metal spatula. Using the tip of a table knife, make wavy ridges in the surface of the cheese at ½-inch intervals, creating a continuous wavy pattern. Press capers into cheese in a decorative pattern. Surround the cheese with radishes and olives.

Yogurt Curd Cheese 1

This delicious soft cheese, called labna in Lebanon and throughout the Middle East, is also well known and loved in many parts of India and the Balkans. It has a fresh and sprightly taste and creamy texture that can fool you into thinking that it has many more calories than it actually does. Left unflavored it makes a wonderful breakfast cheese, but it can also be dressed up with herbs and spices and served with cocktails or fruit.

makes about ¾ cup

2	cups (16 ounces) plain whole-milk yogurt	1	teaspoon salt (optional)

Place a fine mesh strainer over a bowl and line it with four layers of dampened cheesecloth. Put the yogurt in the middle of the cheesecloth and stir in the salt. Bring the corners of the cheesecloth together and twist to make a tight bundle. Secure with string or a rubber band and suspend the sack of yogurt over a bowl (from the handle of a wooden spoon) or from the faucet of the kitchen sink. It should be able to hang undisturbed for 8 hours where it can drip without making a mess. Overnight is ideal. Remove the yogurt cheese to a container and keep refrigerated.

Yogurt Curd Cheese 2

Though similar to yogurt curd cheese 1, the length of time this drains makes it quite different in texture and often in use. As presented here it is delicious with salads or crackers; in the Balkan countries, it is often diced, then deep-fried, and served as a side dish.

4 portions

2½	cups yogurt		1	tablespoon olive oil
1	teaspoon salt		2	teaspoons paprika

Pour the yogurt into a medium-size bowl and stir in the salt. Scald a piece of cheesecloth with boiling water and rinse in cold water. Line a wire sieve with the cheesecloth and place the sieve over a bowl large enough to hold it suspended. Make sure there is plenty of room between the bottom of the sieve and the bottom of the bowl. Pour the yogurt mixture into the sieve. Cover and refrigerate for 48 hours to allow the liquid to drip through.

Remove the strainer and bowl from the refrigerator. Discard the liquid in the bowl. Lifting it by the cheesecloth, invert the cheese onto a work surface. Remove cheesecloth. Shape the cheese into balls or bars, place them on a plate, and sprinkle the olive oil and paprika over them. Refrigerate until serving time.

Yogurt and Cucumber Salad

This salad is both creamy and crunchy and makes a refreshing accompaniment to hot or cold meat dishes.

6 portions

1	cucumber		¼	cup sour cream
2	tablespoons white or malt vinegar		1	teaspoon salt
1	teaspoon sugar		½	teaspoon freshly ground pepper
6	scallions		3	teaspoons chopped fresh dill
1	green bell pepper		1	head of Boston lettuce
1	cup yogurt			

Peel the cucumber and chop fine. Place in a small bowl and add the vinegar and sugar. Set aside for 10 minutes.

Meanwhile, trim the scallions and chop them, using all of the white and 1 inch of the green. Place in a medium-size bowl. Remove the seeds and white membrane from the pepper and chop fine. Add to the scallions. Place the cucumber pieces in a wire sieve and press on them gently with the back of a wooden spoon to extract as much of the liquid as possible. Discard liquid. Add cucumber to the bowl with the vegetables.

In another bowl, combine the yogurt, sour cream, salt, pepper and 2 teaspoons of the dill. Pour the dressing over the vegetables and toss until all the ingredients are well coated.

Remove the dark outer leaves from the Boston lettuce. Separate remaining lettuce into leaves; rinse and dry. Arrange the leaves around the edges of a serving platter. Spoon the yogurt-cucumber mixture into the center. Garnish with the remaining teaspoon of chopped dill.

Danish Blue Salad

This salad makes a nice accompaniment to ham or cold roast chicken. It is also delicious on its own as a light lunch or snack.

2 portions

Dressing

6	tablespoons olive oil
½	teaspoon Dijon-style mustard
2	tablespoons white-wine vinegar
½	teaspoon paprika
½	teaspoon salt
¼	teaspoon freshly ground pepper

Salad

2	ounces Danish blue cheese, at room temperature
2	ounces Cheddar cheese, at room temperature
1	red bell pepper
3	scallions
1	tablespoon chopped fresh dill, or 1½ teaspoons dried dillweed

To prepare the dressing, place the olive oil in a small bowl. Using a fork, gradually beat in the mustard. Beat in the vinegar, then the paprika, salt and pepper.

Cut both cheeses into ¼-inch cubes. Place in a medium-size serving bowl. Halve the pepper and remove the seeds and white membranes. Cut into thin slices and add to the cheeses. Trim the scallions and chop fine, using all of the white part and 1 inch of the green. Add to the cheeses along with the dill. Pour the dressing over the mixture and toss well to blend. Serve at once.

Yogurt Dressing

This dressing is good on salads and makes a delicious accompaniment to kebabs or deep-fried vegetables.

makes about 1½ cups

1	lemon
1	garlic clove
1½	cups yogurt

1	teaspoon salt
1	teaspoon freshly ground pepper

Juice the lemon and place in a screw-top jar of at least 2-cup capacity. Peel and crush the garlic and add to the lemon juice along with the remaining ingredients. Cover jar and shake well to incorporate ingredients. Store in refrigerator until ready to use. Remove garlic just before serving.

Nut and Cream Cheese Balls

These little nuggets make delicious cocktail snacks. They can also be served with a green salad.

makes 16 balls

4	ounces cream cheese, at room temperature
⅛	teaspoon cayenne pepper
1	tablespoon snipped fresh chives

1	tablespoon finely chopped fresh parsley
½	teaspoon salt
¼	teaspoon freshly ground black pepper
2	ounces shelled walnuts

In a small bowl, beat the cream cheese, cayenne, chives, parsley, salt and pepper together with a wooden spoon until the mixture is smooth. Chop the walnuts and stir them into the cheese mixture. Cover loosely and place the bowl in the refrigerator for 30 minutes. When the mixture is firm, shape it into about 16 balls about 1 inch in diameter. Place cheese balls on a serving plate and chill until ready to serve.

Nut and Cream Cheese Puffs

These easy-to-make puffs can be served as a light supper dish, accompanied by a green salad, or as an appetizer with drinks.

makes 8 puffs

8	large Cream Puffs (see Volume 4 Index)	2½	ounces shelled walnuts
8	ounces cream cheese, at room temperature	1	medium-size red bell pepper
2	tablespoons Mayonnaise (see Volume 3 Index)	4	canned pineapple slices
		¼	teaspoon salt

Make the cream puffs. Cool to room temperature.

In a medium-size bowl beat the cream cheese and mayonnaise together until well blended. Chop the walnuts and add to the cheese. Halve the pepper and remove the seeds and white membrane. Chop the pepper fine. Add to the cheese. Drain the pineapple and chop fine. Add pineapple to the cheese along with the salt. Stir until the ingredients are well combined. Set aside.

With a sharp serrated knife, cut a small slice off the tops of the cream puffs. Using a teaspoon, divide the filling evenly among the puffs. Replace the tops, pressing gently so that the tops adhere to the filling. Serve puffs as soon as possible because they will get soggy if allowed to stand.

Part Two

ASPICS, CHAUDFROIDS AND GALANTINES

Aspic, a clear jellied stock, and chaudfroid, an opaque, jellied sauce, are combined and reach the peak of showy elegance in the galantine, a sensationally impressive preparation of boneless meat or fowl, served cold and often elaborately decorated. All three, though delicious in their own right, are essentially intended to add visual delight to the presentation of food.

Aspic, of course, is a clarified stock or consommé that has been made with ingredients that are naturally high in gelatin, such as pig's or calf's feet, or the bones of fish or fowl. Poured in a semijelled state over cold meat and cooled until completely set, it creates a smooth, clear, and, of course, delicious glaze through which the dish proper can be seen, rather like a flower embedded in a glass paperweight.

Set aspic can also be chopped fine and used as a glittering, jewel-like garnish for any number of cold dishes. Or it can be used as a medium to bind together disparate ingredients in a single stunning mold or loaf.

As is often the case in matters culinary, there are a number of theories about the origin of the term "aspic." Some connect it with the asp, and indeed, early molds were often made in the shape of coiled snakes. Others connect it with the Greek word "aspis," meaning buckler, or shield. A more likely connection, perhaps, is with the herb espic, now more commonly known as spikenard, which in the past was often used to flavor the jelly.

Chaudfroid is a combination of aspic and béchamel, velouté, or espagnole sauce. It sets when cold and so makes a decorative and delicious coating for pieces of meat or fish.

One possible origin of the term, which translates simply as "hot-cold," dates back to 1759. The Maréchal de Luxembourg, it seems, was hosting an elaborate dinner that included, among many other delicacies, a fricassee of chicken under a heavy white sauce. Called urgently to the King's Council even as his guests were being seated, the maréchal took his leave, and, having answered the call of duty, returned tired and hungry many hours after the last of the guests had departed. Demanding something to eat at once, he was served some of the fricassee, though reluctantly so, the chef protesting that the hot dish of a few hours earlier was by now cold and the sauce congealed. The result, of course, was found to be delicious, and the name, chaudfroid, was coined on the spot.

Many writers have seen fit to repeat this story, though it should be pointed out that a container unearthed in the ruins of Pompeii and found to harbor remnants of meat in jelly bore the inscription "calidus-frigidus," which also translates as "hot-cold." It seems clear that the general idea, if not the specific dish, predates the hungry maréchal.

At one time chaudfroids (the term refers to the dish itself as well as to the jelled sauce) were rather fancy affairs, with pieces of chicken or other meat arranged on tiered stands made of sculpted bread, then covered with sauce and grandly decorated. Today the presentations are often simpler, but the effect is still always spectacular.

A galantine is a boned, stuffed, and often artfully reshaped fowl or rolled cut of meat that is poached in stock, allowed to cool, and coated with chaudfroid sauce, aspic, or both. The glistening result, often intricately decorated, may rival a Fabergé egg for sheer visual impact.

It is tempting to think that the term "galantine" comes from the Gothic root *gal,* meaning jelly, but it appears more likely that the source is the Old French word for chicken, *galine* (the original dish was made from chicken). Then again, the great French chef Taillevent used the term "galyntyne" to refer to any dish made with the aromatic galingale root, a spice similar to ginger. (The often confusing term "ballottine," refers to a very similar dish, save that, properly speaking, unlike the galantine, it can be served either hot or cold.)

Dishes in aspic and chaudfroids, as should be clear by now, are show pieces, ideal for entertaining when a bit of extra bravura is called for. Though all food should be aesthetically presented, and dishes of any sort can be attractively garnished, the idea here is to create a beautiful object to grace the table or serving board—pleasing first to the eye and secondly, though no less so, to the palate.

To that end it is no accident that these are all cold dishes, since that fact allows (indeed, demands) that they be made well in advance. Without the pressures of last-minute preparation, there is time to indulge in the kind of whimsical or artful decoration that makes each piece uniquely your own.

ASPIC AND CHAUD-FROID

Aspic jelly is a semisolid food made from liquid and gelatin. Gelatin is extracted from the bones of animals and fish. Other gelatinlike substances are extracted from the air bladders of fish (isinglass), from seaweed (agar and carrageen moss), and from fruits and vegetables (pectin). It is the gelatin from bones, however, that is used for molded salads, mousses, and cold soufflés, and to decorate and mold many cold dishes.

Classic aspic is a clear jellied coating of clarified stock or consommé made of ingredients high in natural gelatin such as calf's feet. However, aspic can be made of any good stock with powdered gelatin added; this is usually called "quick aspic." Unflavored powdered gelatin, suitable for all uses, is available in small envelopes, each containing ¼ ounce (7 grams). If you find unflavored gelatin in larger amounts, substitute 1 scant tablespoon for the contents of 1 envelope. This amount of unflavored gelatin will jell 1¾ to 2 cups liquid.

To make quick aspic, the gelatin must first be softened by soaking in cold liquid. For 1 envelope or 1 tablespoon of gelatin, use ¼ cup of cold liquid. Pour the liquid into a small saucepan and sprinkle the gelatin over it. Let it soak for 5 minutes. Then dissolve the gelatin over low heat. Use a rubber spatula to scrape every bit of the gelatin solution into the rest of the recipe liquid, which should be at a bare simmer. Stir until the ingredients are well mixed, otherwise the gelatin may set in rubbery threads. If the aspic is to be used to fill a mold, cool it and pour it into the prepared mold. If it is to be used for a coating or to line a mold, set the saucepan of liquid aspic in a bowl of ice cubes or crushed ice and stir the aspic occasionally as it cools. When it is syrupy and just on the point of setting, it is ready to use for coating.

Chaudfroid, literally translated, means hot-cold. The sauce is made hot but used when cold. While aspic is transparent, chaufroid is opaque. Chaudfroid sauce can be made from a béchamel, velouté or espagnole. It is jellied by adding concentrated aspic made from bones or by adding powdered gelatin. Foods coated with chaudfroid are usually decorated.

Both aspic and chaudfroid can be used for such dishes as cold poached salmon or for simpler dishes such as molded parsleyed ham. Chaudfroid can be used to decorate a whole chicken or individual portions for a simple but elegant meal.

Both of these jellied coatings are invaluable for making plain food look more appetizing and special. When coated in aspic or chaudfroid and decorated tastefully, a dish becomes more impressive. Both of these coatings are also useful as a means of keeping food moist, which makes coated dishes especially suitable for buffet parties.

No special equipment is needed for making aspic or chaudfroid, but if you plan to decorate with aspic, you may wish to acquire aspic cutters, which are small metal cutters in decorative shapes. Other small cutters will do as well, or even a sharp chef's knife used with imagination and a steady hand.

Making Classic Aspic

Make stock or consommé (see Volume 1 Index), using ingredients with a high degree of natural gelatin. These include pig's feet, calf's feet, veal or poultry bones. If you are working with fish, use the heads and skin and the sections around the rib bones. Simmer the liquid and solids long enough to produce a flavorful liquid and, in the case of meat bones, long enough to break down the tissues so that they release gelatin. If you are using a veal knuckle, for instance, it takes 10 to 12 hours for the gelatin in the connective tissues to be completely dissolved. In general, allow at least 5 hours for a well-flavored meat stock that will jell when cold. Fish stock will be flavorful after 30 minutes, but it will not jell without additional gelatin.

To Clarify Stock or Consommé for Aspic. Strain the completed stock to remove all the solids, then strain it again through a fine sieve lined with a double layer of moistened cheesecloth into a bowl. Let the stock cool completely at room temperature, then chill in the refrigerator until any particles of fat have risen to the surface. Carefully lift them off and discard them. Measure the stock and turn it into a heavy saucepan. At this point, if you wish to flavor it with herbs or wine, or to season it with salt and pepper, do so; if added after clarifying, these ingredients can cloud the stock.

Have ready 1 egg white and 1 eggshell for each 2 cups of strained and defatted stock. Crumble the eggshell and beat the egg white lightly until it is well mixed and frothy but not stiff. Add both to the stock and set the saucepan over moderate heat. Stirring constantly, bring the liquid to a boil. Reduce heat to a bare simmer and let the liquid stand over this low heat for 1 hour. As it heats, the egg white and shell will collect the particles remaining in the stock. When the hour is over, use a skimmer to lift the mass of egg white and shell from the surface and discard them. Set a fine sieve over a bowl—preferably a metal one—and line the sieve with several layers of moistened cheesecloth. Ladle—do not pour—the stock through it; if you pour it, the particles that may have settled on the bottom will reenter the stock.

Set the metal bowl of clarified stock in a larger container filled with ice cubes or crushed ice. Stir occasionally to speed the cooling and to permit even jelling; otherwise the outer portions will be set and inner portions still liquid. When cool, the aspic is ready to be poured into molds. If you plan to use it as a coating or to line a mold, continue to chill it, stirring, until it is thickened and is on the point of setting.

Lining a Mold with Aspic

Using Aspic

Aspic jelly can be used to line any mold; when turned out, the molded food will have a transparent coating to keep the ingredients moist and delicious and to give them an elegant appearance. Choose a mold just large enough for the ingredients: a charlotte mold, soufflé dish, deep cake pan, or molds specially designed for aspics can be used. It is easier to use a plain mold. In a fancy mold the aspic will get into nooks and crannies and will be more difficult—though not impossible—to turn out. Molds can be oiled with almond oil, but this may spoil the transparent surface. Or they can be rinsed with cold water before being lined or filled. It is better to do neither, but to have an absolutely clean mold, free of any fat. Chill the mold for about an hour either in a container of crushed ice, in the coldest part of the refrigerator or for about ½ hour in the freezer. When you're ready to begin, the aspic should be cool and on the point of setting. If it is too thin, it will not solidify on the sides but will run down to the bottom. If it is too thick, the lining will be lumpy and uneven. The aspic is just right when it has the consistency of an egg white. It will quiver slightly when shaken, rather than slop around like a liquid.

Pour about 2 tablespoons of aspic into the mold and immediately swirl the mold around to spread the aspic over the sides. Because the mold is cold, the aspic will congeal almost at once. Continue to add liquid aspic, swirling the mold as you do, until the sides of the mold are evenly coated. Do not worry about coating the base; once the sides are coated you won't have any problem doing it.

If you wish to set decorations in the sides and base of the mold, prepare the decorations and chill them. When the lining layer of aspic is firm, pick up one piece of decoration at a time with tweezers, dip it into the liquid aspic, and place it on the firm aspic. Continue with other pieces and arrange in a decorative pattern. When decorating the sides, you may need to tilt the mold and let each section set before turning and

1 Chill clarified aspic to the point of setting, that is, to the consistency of egg white, before using it.

2 To line a mold, first chill the mold for 1 hour in a bowl of ice cubes, the refrigerator or the freezer.

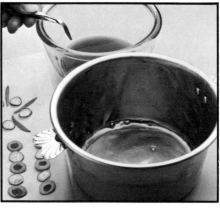

5 Cut fruits, vegetables or herbs into small decorative shapes. Pick up with tweezers and dip into setting aspic.

6 Arrange the shapes on the base in a decorative pattern and chill to set. To decorate sides, work in sections.

9 For piped chopped aspic, chop very small. Make a paper piping bag and cut off the tip. Spoon aspic into the bag.

10 Pipe a thin line of chopped aspic around small mousses or individual portions of meat, fish or poultry.

3 Pour 2 tablespoons aspic into the mold and swirl the mold until the aspic jells on the sides. Pour out excess.

4 Continue until sides are completely coated. Spoon a little aspic into the base to coat it evenly.

7 To chop aspic, pour into a baking pan and chill to set. Wet a sheet of wax paper and turn out the pan of aspic.

8 Use a wet knife to cut the aspic across, then diagonally. Use the whole knife blade, not just the point.

11 To make decorative shapes, set aspic in a baking pan. Cut out shapes with aspic cutters or a sharp knife.

12 Use aspic shapes to decorate dishes coated with chaudfroid sauce. Use a spatula to pick up the individual shapes.

decorating the next part. When the decorating pieces are firmly in place, carefully pour in another layer of clear aspic, just as you did for the lining, so that the decorations are covered. This will set them even more securely so they will not move out of place when you pour in the mousse or other jellied filling.

Good decorations can be made from pieces of pimiento, thin slivers of orange and lemon rind, slivers of celery, cutouts of green or yellow bell pepper, cooked small pasta shapes, blanched herb leaves. Flower centers can be made from cooked egg yolk, petals from cooked egg white, and stems from scallion leaves.

Filling and Unmolding Aspic Molds

When the lining and any decorations are firmly set, spoon or pour the filling into the mold; do this carefully so you do not dislodge the decorations. The filling—mousse or soufflé mixture, salad or whatever—must also be cool and on the point of setting. Fill the mold to the top, smooth it, cover with plastic wrap, and refrigerate. If the mold does not have a flat bottom, be sure to set it on crumpled foil to keep it level. Chill the mold for the amount of time specified in the recipe.

When you are ready to unmold the aspic, have ready the platter or plate on which you are going to serve it; rinse the plate with cold water so that, if necessary, you can slide the aspic to center it. Insert the point of a knife along the edge of the mold to loosen it and allow air to get between the aspic and the mold, then dip the bottom of the mold into a pan of hot water for 1 second. Wipe the mold, then put the platter or plate on top of it and, holding them firmly together, turn the mold and plate over. If the mold is not released, you may repeat the dipping process, but another method is easier: Wrap the upside-down mold in a cloth dipped in hot water and wrung out; after a few seconds the aspic should slide out readily. Lift the mold away, and carefully blot up any water or any melted aspic. Put the plate in the refrigerator until ready to serve.

Decorating with Aspic

Chopped Aspic. A shimmering border of chopped aspic looks attractive around a jellied dish. Pour liquid aspic into a clean grease-free baking pan and chill it until firm. Put a sheet of wax paper on a chopping board and brush it with cold water. The cold water prevents sticking. Use the point of a knife to release the aspic from the edge of the pan and turn it out on the wax paper. Chop the aspic with a large stainless-steel knife, using the whole blade. Cut first in one direction, then diagonally to achieve a diamond effect, which makes the aspic sparkle more.

To use the aspic diamonds, simply spoon them around the base of the main dish. For individual portions, the aspic must be chopped very fine. It can be spooned or piped onto the plates. To pipe it, make a paper piping bag and cut a tiny piece off the end to make a small hole. Spoon aspic into the bag, then pipe it around the food. The fine line of aspic piping gives a glistening border.

Aspic Shapes. Aspic shapes make attractive decorations for cold dishes, even those otherwise not made with gelatin. To make them, chill the aspic as described under Chopped Aspic. When it is turned out, use a sharp knife or aspic cutters to make small cubes, triangles, diamonds, rounds, etc. Dip either knife or cutter into cold water before each use. To move the little shapes, slide them onto a thin metal spatula.

Layered Molds. Layered aspic molds are easy to make and have become popular as a first course. Pour a base of aspic into a mold, then add a layer of chopped meat, poultry, fish, vegetables or mousse. Add another layer of aspic. Continue layering in this way, ending with a layer of aspic. If the last layer is to be the top of the dish, it can be decorated. If it is to be the bottom, unmold the layered mixture and decorate after unmolding.

Aspic Topping and Coating. Aspic can be used as a thin coating on meat, poultry and fish. For coating, the aspic must be at the "egg-white" stage and the food to be coated should be very cold and the surface free of grease. Use a very supple brush or a feather to apply a thin coating. Chill the food and apply a second coating, or more if needed, chilling after each layer. When decorations are added, they must be attached with some liquid aspic and, after setting, should be covered with more liquid aspic. If you are working with a sturdy food that keeps its shape such as a piece of meat or a whole bird, this coating can be done on a tray and the food can be transferred to the serving platter when you have completed preparing it. If you are working with a fragile food such as a fish, it must be done on the serving platter so the fish will not need to be moved.

Aspic can also be poured over the top of a mousse or a pâté and decorations can be set in the aspic layer.

Mayonnaise Collée

Mayonnaise can be turned into a coating sauce or the base for a mousse by adding aspic or gelatin. The amount of mayonnaise to make depends on the amount of food to be coated. A mixture of 1 cup mayonnaise and 4 tablespoons gelatin solution will coat about 6 individual portions, or a whole bird or fish that will make 4 portions. For 1 cup of homemade mayonnaise (see Volume 3 Index), soften 1 envelope or 1 scant tablespoon powdered gelatin in 4 tablespoons cold water for 5 minutes as described for quick aspic. Set the saucepan over low heat and dissolve the gelatin until the solution is clear. Let the solution cool, then beat it into the mayonnaise. For more flavor, the gelatin can be dissolved in stock and wine flavored with herbs. To use already prepared aspic jelly for a mayonnaise collée, make it somewhat stiffer than usual. Use 6 tablespoons of the liquid jelly for 1 cup mayonnaise. If it is already jelled, melt it and let it cool to room temperature before beating it

into the mayonnaise. The gelatin mixture and the mayonnaise can also be combined in a blender.

To use mayonnaise collée as a coating sauce, place the food to be coated on a wire rack set over a platter. The food should be cold and the mayonnaise collée on the point of setting. Spoon or brush the coating over the food, letting any excess drip onto the platter. These excess drops can be scraped up, melted if necessary, cooled again, and used. When an even coating has been applied, the surface can be decorated in the same way as a chaudfroid (see below).

Mayonnaise collée makes a good base for a vegetable mousse. Simply stir chopped vegetables mixed with shellfish, meat or poultry into the mayonnaise, spoon into a mold, and chill until set.

Chaudfroid

Chaudfroid is not transparent but is an opaque sauce mixed with aspic, which makes the sauce set when cold. The process of making a chaudfroid is similar to that for making a mayonnaise collée.

If the chaudfroid is made with classic aspic, the aspic must be very stiff, or extra gelatin will be needed. If adding extra gelatin, the usual proportions for making it are ½ cup liquid aspic and 1 teaspoon powdered gelatin for 1½ cups sauce. If you are jelling a white sauce with powdered gelatin alone, allow 1 tablespoon gelatin for 1 cup sauce plus ½ cup cream. The type of sauce and the color can be varied to suit the food you are coating. White chaudfroid is made from béchamel or velouté (see Volume 3 Index), brown chaudfroid from espagnole (see Volume 3 Index); both béchamel and velouté can be colored with tomato purée, spinach purée, or carrot purée, and can be flavored with herbs or spices.

To make the sauce with aspic jelly, soak the extra gelatin in the liquid aspic for 5 minutes, then dissolve over low heat. Do not let the aspic boil or it will become rubbery. If the sauce is

Using Chaudfroid Sauce

makes about 2 cups

1	teaspoon unflavored gelatin, if needed
½	cup liquid aspic stock
1½	cups Béchamel or Velouté Sauce (see Volume 3 Index)

1 If aspic needs to be stiffened (see Chaudfroid in Introduction), soak gelatin in aspic for 5 minutes. Dissolve gelatin over low heat and cool slightly.

2 Pour aspic in a thin stream into béchamel or velouté, whisking all the time so that it is evenly distributed.

3 Cool the sauce until it will coat the back of a wooden spoon. Stir from time to time during cooling.

4 Place chicken or fish portions or chops on a wire rack with a tray underneath.

5 Pour the sauce onto the center of the food. When it has run down and completely coated the sides, stop pouring.

6 To coat a whole chicken, anchor it to the wire rack by passing a skewer from under the rack through the body.

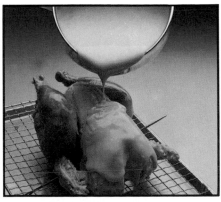

7 Pour the sauce over the top of the bird, first tilting and pouring along one side.

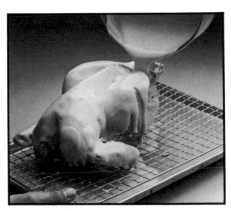

8 Keeping the movement continuous, pour down the other side, making sure to overlap the first pouring. The chicken should be evenly coated with sauce.

1 Cut shapes with a sharp stainless-steel knife. Cut squares, diamonds, triangles, crescents, half-moons and strips.

2 Abstract geometric designs can be made with diamond and half-moon shapes. These are best for small portions.

3 Use strips of cucumber skin for flowers, orange or lemon rind for stems. Use aspic cutters for various shapes.

4 Arrange designs on wax paper so that they are ready to be used immediately.

5 Decorate a fish along its length with a trail of flowers or with a row of overlapping cucumber slices.

6 Radish or olive crescents or halves make an attractive border. Use tweezers to position them.

cool, place it over low heat. Pour in the aspic solution in a thin stream, stirring all the time. Cool the sauce until it will coat the back of a wooden spoon. Stir from time to time to prevent formation of lumps. Use the sauce as soon as it has reached the coating stage.

To make the white chaudfroid sauce with powdered gelatin alone, soften 1 envelope or 1 scant tablespoon powdered gelatin in 4 tablespoons water, then dissolve it in 1 cup boiling velouté sauce, stirring all the time. Remove sauce from the heat and stir in ½ cup heavy cream. Taste and add seasoning if necessary. Strain the

sauce into a metal bowl and let it cool, stirring.

To make brown chaudfroid sauce with gelatin alone, stir the softened gelatin into 1 cup of reduced espagnole sauce enriched with 1 tablespoon of meat glaze. Stir well. Strain the sauce into a metal bowl and flavor it with 1 tablespoon Madeira wine. Let the sauce cool, stirring as usual.

Using Chaudfroid. The main use of chaudfroid is to coat cold meat, poultry and fish. Boned cooked chicken or turkey roll are easier for beginners as there are no crevices for the sauce to fall into. Ham can be coated,

as can small cooked game birds such as quails or partridges. Individual portions of chicken, turkey, game or lamb chops are also suitable. Whole fish, such as a large salmon for a buffet centerpiece, or trout or portions of fish to be eaten cold are particularly good.

If you are coating a whole bird or poultry portions, remove the skin first. The skin of birds is rough and would spoil the smooth appearance of the completed dish. Place the bird on a wire rack set over a tray and pour the sauce in one continuous movement to avoid ridges and patches. If there is any possibility of the bird's sliding around, anchor it to the rack with a skewer. The decorations used on whole birds can be larger and more impressive than those used on individual portions.

If you are coating chicken portions, fish steaks or chops, which are easiest to begin with, pour the sauce in a thin stream onto the center of the food. As soon as it runs down and coats the sides, stop pouring. If you pour too much sauce, you will get an uneven finish. Chill in the refrigerator for about 2 hours to set the coating. Decorate and, if desired, coat with clear aspic.

When preparing fish, coat them on their serving platter because fish are too delicate to lift without breaking. Poach a whole salmon or trout or individual portions of fish. While the fish is still warm, carefully peel off the skin. If you are working with salmon, let it cool completely after skinning, then remove the thin layer of dark-colored meat to give the fish a better appearance. Pour on the chaudfroid when the fish is completely cold.

Decorating Chaudfroid and Aspic

Prepare decorations in advance and arrange on a sheet of wax paper; otherwise the jellied coating will set before you can get the decorations in place.
• *Cucumber skin.* Cut into thin slivers to make flower stems, but do not use bigger pieces because the skin is indigestible.
• *Tarragon leaves.* Use young tender leaves as flower petals or leaves.
• *Radishes.* Slice paper-thin for rounds; cut into halves and then slice to make patterns with semicircles.
• *Tomato skin.* Peel off strips of skin and curl them to make roses, or cut out pieces to make designs.
• *Hard-cooked egg yolk.* Slice and cut into designs; or crumble to make flower centers. To make larger egg-yolk cutouts, combine 1 cup liquid aspic jelly with the hard-cooked yolks of 6 eggs and process in a blender or food processor. Pour into a baking pan about 8 × 6 inches and chill to set.
• *Hard-cooked egg white.* Chop egg white into small bits for a white decora-

tion. To make larger egg white cutouts, strain the whites to remove the ligaments, then poach whites in a large flat pan of water. When cool, cut the sheet of egg white with aspic cutters.
• *Olives.* Pitted black and green olives, plain or stuffed, can be sliced crosswise and used as circles in a design. Black olives are sometimes halved lengthwise and can be used to represent black grapes.
• *Pimientos.* These canned roasted peppers are used for their beautiful red color and are easy to cut into strips or fancy shapes.
• *Gherkins.* These tiny pickles can be cut into fans or slices.
• *Lemon or orange peel.* Cut thin slivers of either to give attractive color and taste. Grated rind may be used for flower centers.

There are many other things that make good edible decorations. Once you have started to use your imagination, the possibilities will entrance you.

Cutting Decorations. Use a very sharp stainless-steel knife: sharp to insure that your designs have clean edges, and stainless so flavors will not be transferred from knife to food.

Cut a strip of aspic and then from the strip cut diamond shapes, squares, rectangles and triangles. These can be used for geometric designs. Or cut small diamonds and use them for flower petals. Use strips of cucumber skin or scallion greens for flower stems.

Crescents can be cut from citrus rinds, stuffed or whole black olives, pimiento strips or cucumber. To make a border design with crescents, arrange them alternately—curved side in, curved side out. Half-moons can be used in the same way.

Apply decorations carefully. Use tweezers or a thin skewer to lift the decoration and then dip it into a little liquid aspic that is almost on the point of setting. Place the decoration on the coating surface. When all the pieces are in place, let the dish chill until the decorations are firmly set. Then, for a perfect finish, coat the entire surface with a thin layer of clear aspic. Spoon it on, or brush it on with a feather pastry brush.

GALAN-TINES

A galantine is a boned roll of uncooked meat, stuffed with a well-flavored and substantial mixture, poached in stock, cooled, and finally coated with aspic or chaudfroid or a layer of each. The process sounds complicated, and this is not a quick dish to prepare. However, the individual steps are not difficult. It is sensible to start making a galantine at least a day before it is needed so it can be cooled to room temperature and chilled overnight. The cooked galantine can be stored in its wrappings for up to 3 days.

A galantine provides a perfect centerpiece for a buffet. It is an elegant dish that demands careful preparation but no last-minute attention. Since the meat or poultry is completely boneless, it is easy to carve and serve. Originally only poultry was used in a galantine, but eventually other birds and cuts of meat were adopted. Turkey, game birds, veal, pork and beef can be used. No sauce is needed to accompany a galantine since it is already coated with a sauce in jellied form. A delicate garnish of fresh fruit or vegetables is all that is needed for decoration.

There are three principal ingredients in a poultry galantine: the bird, the stuffing and the coating. You will also need stock (made from the carcass and giblets) in which to poach the bird and the fruits and vegetables you plan to use for garnish.

The Bird. If you are serving many people, your first choice should be a turkey. Once sliced, a galantine will dry out, so plan carefully, choosing a turkey just large enough for the number of guests. If you are serving a small number of people, choose a chicken, duck or game bird. A frozen bird can be used successfully in a galantine. The stuffing adds ample flavor and there is no danger of the flesh becoming dry since the galantine is poached. This is an excellent method for cooking birds that may no longer be in their prime. The cooking can be extended for an older and tougher bird to insure tender results.

Frozen birds are always sold oven-ready with the giblets inside. Thaw the bird in its wrappings in the refrigerator. When the bird is completely thawed, remove the giblets and set them aside. Rinse the bird with cold water.

The Stuffing. The stuffing for a galantine is always substantial. Because meat that is chilled is usually somewhat dry, the stuffing must be moist. Minced meat, including pork or pork sausage meat, veal, and small amounts of ham or bacon, is used (the amount of ham or bacon is limited so its strong flavor does not overwhelm the flavor of the other ingredients). The mixture is seasoned, flavored with herbs and a little onion, and moistened with Cognac or a fortified wine such as Madeira or sherry.

Sometimes the flavoring meat is cut into strips rather than minced; the strips are arranged between two layers of stuffing to give a decorative effect when the galantine is sliced. Ham and tongue, because of their color, are often used this way. Many variations on the basic stuffing mixture are possible.

The Coating. A galantine can be coated with aspic, with a chaudfroid sauce, or with a glaze of clear aspic over a coat of chaudfroid. The stock in which the bird is poached is used to make the aspic. If the stock does not set when chilled, some powdered gelatin can be added. The amount needed depends on the amount of natural gelatin in the stock. Because too much gelatin would make the aspic stiff, perhaps even rubbery, start with ½ envelope gelatin for 2 cups liquid, or half the customary amount. Soften the gelatin and dissolve it in the hot stock. Cool the mixture over ice, then spoon about 2 tablespoons of it onto a flat plate and refrigerate it. As soon as the stock is completely cold—in about 10 minutes—it should jell. If it is not firm,

start again, adding more gelatin to the stock. When the galantine is completed, the opaque chaudfroid and the clear aspic must be firm enough to be sliced with the meat.

The bird must be completely cold before it is coated—if the bird or sauce were warm, the coating would not set—and the aspic or chaudfroid must be on the point of setting. If you plan to finish the galantine with an aspic glaze, apply it only after the chaudfroid coating is firmly set.

The Garnish. Fresh fruit, vegetables and many other foods can be used to garnish the top of a galantine. Strips of citrus peel, anchovies, cucumber skin, radish slices, whole cloves, capers, sliced gherkins, olives and celery are some of the possibilities. Strips and thin slices are best, as they can be secured firmly and do not make the carving difficult. See Decorating Chaudfroid and Aspic. Garnishes for a chaudfroid coating should be arranged in the coating before it is completely set. Those for an aspic coating should be attached with a little liquid aspic. When the garnishes are completely set, spoon a final coating of clear aspic over all.

Making a Galantine

Because of the substantial stuffing, a galantine is a good way to stretch a single bird to serve a larger number of people. And because the dish is boneless and therefore completely edible, portions do not have to be too large. The larger the bird, the higher the proportion of meat to bone. Small birds weighing up to 5 pounds provide about 2½ pounds of meat when boned; larger, heavier birds yield meat in an increasing ratio. However, birds over 10 pounds are not suitable for this preparation: They will be too large to handle easily when stuffed, and it will be difficult to cook the bird through without overcooking the outside portions.

The weight of the stuffing can be as much as half of the weight of the boned meat. For example, a 5-pound chicken boned to yield about 2½

pounds meat can be combined with up to 1¼ pounds stuffing. Allowing about 6 ounces per portion, this will serve about 10 people.

Boning the Bird. Bone the bird so that the skin and flesh are in one piece (see Volume 8 Index). The most important thing is not to tear the skin—although very small tears can be dealt with. It is the skin that keeps the stuffing intact. Any small pieces of flesh separated during the boning process can be added to the stuffing. If you like, the thicker portions such as the breasts can be removed carefully, cut into strips, and then layered in the stuffing. Always use a very sharp knife for the boning and save all bones and trimmings for the stock. Cover the boned bird lightly and refrigerate it until you are ready to stuff it. You can bone a turkey, duck or game bird in the same fashion as a chicken, but the large size of the turkey will make it a little harder to handle. Small game birds will also be slightly more difficult to handle because of their size.

Making Stock and Stuffing. Use the carcass and other bones plus gizzards, heart and neck to make stock (see Volume 1 Index). Do not use the liver as it clouds the stock. Allow ample time for the making of the stock, so that the flavors and the gelatin content of the bones will be released. When the stock is cooked, strain and degrease it.

While the stock is simmering, prepare the stuffing. Remove and discard any skin, bone or cartilage from the stuffing meats and mince the meats. Peel and mince the onion and other flavoring vegetables. Mix the stuffing well, cover with plastic wrap, and refrigerate until ready to use.

Trim and slice any ingredients that are to be layered in the galantine.

Stuffing and Cooking the Bird. Take the bird from the refrigerator and spread it out flat, skin down, on the work surface. Season the inside with salt and pepper. Spread the stuffing evenly down the center, and arrange any solid ingredients (strips of ham or breast meat, sliced olives, pistachios, etc.) between two layers of stuffing.

Thread a trussing needle with fine

string or strong cotton thread. Draw the edges of the skin together and stitch to form a compact roll. Wrap the roll in a double layer of cheesecloth or in a sheet of muslin and tie the ends securely.

Pour the strained and degreased stock into a pan just large enough to hold the galantine, and immerse the roll in the stock. Be sure it is completely covered; if not, add more stock, or water if there is no stock. Cover the pan and simmer the galantine for the time specified in the individual recipe.

Cooling and Pressing the Galantine. Lift the cooked galantine by the ends of the cheesecloth or muslin and let it drain over the pan for a few seconds. Transfer it to a large plate. Reserve the stock. When the galantine is cool enough to handle, tighten the wrappings or remove them and roll it in clean cheesecloth or muslin and tie securely. Put the galantine between two plates and place a weight on top. The weight should be sufficient to press the galantine and firm the contents but should not be so heavy that it causes juices to escape. Cool the galantine at room temperature until it is completely cool to the touch, then refrigerate in the wrappings until ready to proceed.

Coating the Galantine. Use the reserved stock to make aspic; test for jelling and add more gelatin if needed. Take the chilled roll from the refrigerator and remove the wrappings and the trussing string or thread. Place the roll on a wire rack set over a tray or large plate. If you are using chaudfroid, pour an even coating of the sauce over the bird and chill the galantine in the refrigerator for 2 hours, or until the sauce is set. If you are using aspic, brush a thin coating over the galantine and let that set. Then add the decorations, attaching them with a dab of aspic that is on the point of setting. When the decorations are firm, apply another layer of aspic, or several thin layers if you find that easier, and chill the galantine in the refrigerator for 2 hours, or until set. If you wish to apply an aspic glaze over a coating of chaudfroid, be sure the chaudfroid has set firmly before you proceed.

Serving a Galantine. A whole galantine makes a handsome centerpiece for a buffet table. Arrange it on a serving platter with a simple garnish of chopped aspic and watercress sprigs around it.

Although the galantine can be carved easily after guests are assembled, you may prefer to carve it before guests arrive. If so, arrange the slices on a serving dish, apply an even coating of aspic over the slices, and chill until set. This makes serving very simple and the meat is kept moist and delicious. Garnish the serving dish and/or each separate slice.

Chicken Galantine

6 to 8 portions

1   oven-ready roasting chicken, 4 pounds

Stock

1½   pounds knuckle of veal, chopped and blanched
2   large carrots, quartered
2   Spanish onions, quartered
1   leek, sliced
1   celery rib, sliced
1   Bouquet Garni (see Volume 1 Index)
6   white peppercorns

Coating

1   envelope (1 scant tablespoon) unflavored gelatin
7   black olives
    strips of cucumber skin

Stuffing

8   ounces boneless veal
6   ounces boneless lean ham
4   ounces sausage meat
½   cup fresh white bread crumbs
1   tablespoon chopped fresh parsley
2   teaspoons chopped fresh sage or 1 teaspoon dried
2   tablespoons lemon juice
    grated rind of ½ lemon
    salt and freshly ground pepper
    large pinch of grated nutmeg
1   egg, beaten

Variations: For spicy stuffing, omit herbs and add a pinch of ground allspice, a pinch of grated nutmeg. Add 6 tablespoons chopped pistachios and 3 tablespoons sliced stuffed green olives.

• For poultry stuffing for game birds, replace the veal with boned chicken meat; marinate the minced meats in 2 tablespoons Madeira wine and 2 tablespoons brandy for 2 hours. Use thyme instead of sage.

• Make a mushroom stuffing by sautéing 6 ounces chopped mushrooms and adding them, along with 6 chopped pitted black olives, to the basic mixture.

• To make an orange-flavored stuffing, substitute 2 tablespoons orange juice and the grated rind of 1 orange for the lemon juice and lemon rind.

• For fruit stuffing, add 4 ounces chopped pitted dates, the peeled segments of an orange and 4 tablespoons chopped walnuts to the orange stuffing (see above).

1 Bone the chicken (see Volume 8 Index). Cover and refrigerate.

2 Use the bones, giblets and other stock ingredients to make 7 cups of stock (see Volume 1 Index).

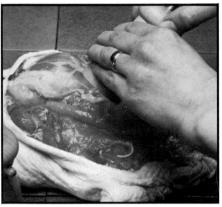

6 Spread the boned chicken out flat, skin down, on a work surface. Season flesh with salt and pepper.

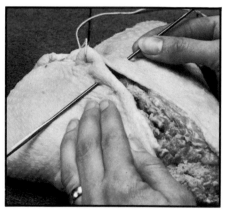

7 Spread stuffing evenly over the center of the chicken. Draw edges together and sew to make a compact roll.

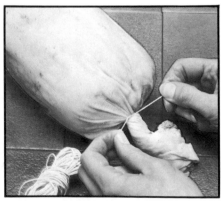

11 When galantine is cool enough to handle, tighten the wrappings, or renew wrappings and tie tight.

12 Put the galantine between 2 plates and put a weight on top. Chill until it is completely cold.

13 Remove wrappings and trussing strings. Put galantine on a wire rack set over a plate or tray.

3 While the stock is simmering, make the stuffing. Mince or grind the veal and ham.

4 Mix minced meat with sausage meat, bread crumbs, herbs, lemon juice and grated rind.

5 Season stuffing mixture generously. Add the nutmeg and beaten egg, and mix well.

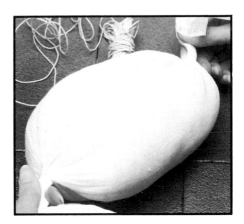

8 Wrap the galantine in a double layer of cheesecloth and tie ends together to make a tight roll.

9 Strain the stock into a saucepan and immerse the galantine. Cover and simmer for 1½ hours.

10 When galantine is cooked, drain it over the pan and set aside to cool slightly. Reserve the stock.

14 Use some of the stock to make 2½ cups aspic. Add gelatin if necessary. Cool the aspic. Brush a thin coat on the galantine.

15 Halve and pit olives. Dip pieces of garnish into the aspic and arrange in place. Chill until set.

16 Pour aspic along the top of the galantine and let it run down to coat the bird completely. Chill until set.

Quick Aspic

makes about 2½ cups

1	cup degreased stock	1	lemon
½	cup dry sherry	6	black peppercorns
½	cup dry white wine	1	teaspoon salt
1	onion	1	egg
1	carrot	¼	cup cold water
1	celery rib	4	teaspoons unflavored gelatin

Pour all the liquids into a large saucepan. Peel and quarter the onion. Scrape and halve the carrot and the celery rib. Grate the rind from the lemon. Add the vegetables to the pan along with grated lemon rind and juice, peppercorns and salt. Simmer for about 30 minutes.

Separate the egg, reserving the yolk for another use. Beat the egg white until frothy and crush the egg shell. Add both to the stock, whisking constantly while bringing the liquid to a boil. Reduce heat to a simmer and let the stock simmer for 30 minutes. Lift off the egg-white mass with a skimmer. Ladle the stock through a fine sieve lined with a double layer of moistened cheesecloth into a clean saucepan. Pour the ¼ cup cold water into a cup and sprinkle the gelatin on top. Soak for 5 minutes. Scrape the gelatin into the stock and stir over low heat until the gelatin is completely dissolved. Cool the aspic until it is on the point of setting.

Jellied Green Mayonnaise

makes about 1 cup

1½	tablespoons well-drained puréed spinach	½	teaspoon minced fresh watercress
½	teaspoon minced fresh tarragon	1	cup Mayonnaise (see Volume 3 Index)
½	teaspoon minced fresh parsley	¼	cup cold water
		1	envelope (1 scant tablespoon) unflavored gelatin

Stir the spinach purée, tarragon, parsley and watercress into the mayonnaise. Pour the cold water into a small saucepan and sprinkle the gelatin over it. Soak for 5 minutes. Set the saucepan over low heat and dissolve the softened gelatin, stirring all the time, until it is clear and no granules remain on the sides of the pan. Let the gelatin cool. Beat the gelatin into the mayonnaise until well combined. Chill the mayonnaise, stirring from time to time, until it is on the point of setting. It is ready to use when it will coat the back of a wooden spoon.

Galantine of Pheasant

4 portions

1	pheasant, 2½ pounds		salt and freshly ground pepper
4	ounces boneless veal		
6	ounces boneless ham	3	tablespoons Madeira wine
½	slice white bread	1	teaspoon unflavored gelatin (optional)
1	small onion		
2	teaspoons chopped fresh sage	½	orange
			watercress sprigs
1	tablespoon chopped fresh parsley		

Have the pheasant dressed and all viscera removed. Wipe the bird inside and out with a damp cloth. Bone the bird (see Volume 8 Index), keeping the skin in one piece. Use the bones and giblets to make 3 cups Game Stock (see Volume 8 Index). While the stock is simmering, make the stuffing. Mince the veal and ham. Whirl the bread in a blender or processor to make ¼ cup crumbs. Add to the meat. Peel and mince the onion. Add onion and herbs to the meats and season well with salt and pepper. Pour in the Madeira. Mix well. Sauté a bit of the mixture and adjust the flavor if necessary with more herbs and salt.

Spread the pheasant, skin side down, on a work surface. Season the meat side with salt and pepper. Spoon the stuffing evenly down the center. Draw the edges of the bird together to form a roll and sew the edges together with a trussing needle and strong cotton thread or fine string. Wrap the galantine in a double layer of cheesecloth or a muslin cloth and tie the ends. Place the galantine in a pan large enough to hold it and pour in enough stock to cover it completely. Cover the pan. Set the pan over low heat and bring to a simmer; simmer the galantine for 1 hour. Remove the roll from the stock, let it drain over the pan for a few seconds, then set it aside until cool enough to handle. Reserve the stock.

When the galantine is cool, tighten the wrapping or rewrap the galantine in clean cheesecloth or muslin, tying it tightly. Top the galantine with a plate and a weight; leave it at room temperature until completely cold. Store it in its wrappings, lightly covered, in the refrigerator until ready to continue.

Use the cold stock to make 1 cup aspic. Test for jelling. If more gelatin is needed, sprinkle the gelatin over 4 tablespoons of the still-liquid aspic to soften. Leave for 5 minutes while heating remaining aspic. Add softened gelatin and stir to dissolve. Cool the aspic over a bowl of crushed ice. Unwrap the galantine and remove trussing strings. Use a sharp knife to carve the roll into even slices. Arrange the slices in an overlapping pattern on a serving platter. When the aspic is on the point of setting, spoon it over the slices, coating them completely. Transfer the dish to the refrigerator and chill for 2 hours, or until the aspic is set.

When ready to serve, peel and slice the orange and arrange the slices at one end of the platter, or around the aspic-glazed slices of meat, according to the size and shape of the platter. Garnish with the watercress sprigs.

Brown Chaudfroid Sauce

makes about 1¼ cups

1½	cups Sauce Espagnole (see Volume 3 Index)	2	tablespoons cold water	
1	tablespoon meat glaze, homemade or purchased*	1	envelope (1 scant tablespoon) unflavored gelatin	
		1	tablespoon Madeira wine	

Pour the sauce into a saucepan and add the meat glaze. Simmer the sauce over moderate heat until reduced to about 1 cup. Put the cold water in a cup and sprinkle 1 teaspoon of the gelatin over it. Soak gelatin for 5 minutes, then scrape it into the hot sauce and stir until softened gelatin is completely dissolved and mixed with the sauce. Pour 2 tablespoons of the sauce onto a plate and refrigerate it until it is completely cold, about 10 minutes. The sauce should be jelled; if not, repeat the process with another teaspoon of gelatin. Repeat again if sauce does not jell. Do not add too much; the sauce should be silky, not stiff. When the sauce has enough gelatin to become firm, stir in the Madeira and let the sauce cool over crushed ice, stirring often, until on the point of setting. Use brown chaudfroid as soon as it is ready.

*Meat glaze, or *glace de viande*, is beef stock reduced to a very thick jelly-like substance. The nearest commercially available equivalent, though far less good, is beef extract, available in specialty stores and many supermarkets.

Chicken Livers in Aspic

6 portions

1	head of crisp lettuce	2	tablespoons butter	
6	whole chicken livers	¼	teaspoon salt	
1	large onion	⅛	teaspoon freshly ground white pepper	
2½	cups clarified aspic, made from chicken stock	½	cup sherry	

Wash and dry the lettuce, then shred it. Roll in a towel and refrigerate until ready to serve. Rinse the livers, separate into halves, and remove any bits of membrane or green areas. Dry the livers with paper towels. Peel and mince the onion. Melt the aspic, but keep it cool.

Rinse a 4-cup mold. Pour in enough aspic to make a ½-inch layer on the bottom. Chill the mold in the refrigerator until the aspic is set. Melt the butter in a skillet over moderate heat. Add the minced onions and sauté them, stirring frequently, for 5 minutes. Add the livers and sauté them, shaking the pan, until the livers are lightly browned all over.

Sprinkle the salt and pepper over the livers. Pour the sherry into the pan, cover, and simmer over low heat for 10 minutes. Use a slotted spoon to transfer the livers to a plate. Increase heat to high under the skillet and boil the liquid until it is syrupy. Coat the livers with the syrupy liquid and set them aside to cool.

When the livers are cool, place them on top of the set aspic in the mold. Fill the mold with remaining aspic and return it to the refrigerator. Chill for 3 hours, or until set. Unmold the aspic on a flat serving dish and surround with the chilled shredded lettuce.

Chicken and Vegetables in Aspic

6 portions

1	roasting chicken, 4 pounds	1	cup dry white wine	
2	medium-size onions	2	cups Chicken Stock (see Volume 1 Index) or canned broth	
1	green pepper			
2	large carrots			
4	celery ribs	½	teaspoon dried thyme	
1	lemon	½	teaspoon dried rosemary	
5	black peppercorns	1	bay leaf	
4	tablespoons vegetable oil	2	parsley sprigs	
3	garlic cloves	1	teaspoon salt	

Cut the chicken into 8 pieces. Peel and slice the onion; separate the slices into rings. Wash the pepper, cut out the stem, and scoop out seeds and ribs. Cut the pepper into rings. Scrape the carrots and slice into chunks or spears. Trim, string and slice the celery. Cut the lemon into thin slices and remove any seeds. Crush the peppercorns.

Heat the oil in a large flameproof casserole over moderate heat. When oil is hot, add the chicken pieces and sauté for 5 minutes on each side, until lightly browned all over. Use a slotted spoon to transfer chicken from the casserole to a plate. Peel the garlic and put through a press into the oil remaining in the casserole. Add onion rings, pepper rings, carrots and celery to the casserole. Sauté, stirring frequently, for 5 to 7 minutes, until onions are soft and translucent but not browned. Remove vegetables to a plate. Pour the wine and chicken stock into the casserole and add the lemon slices, herbs, crushed peppercorns and salt. Increase heat to high and bring the liquid to a boil. Return chicken pieces to the casserole and cover. Reduce heat to low and simmer for 1¼ hours. Return vegetables to the casserole and simmer for 15 to 30 minutes longer, until chicken and vegetables are very tender.

Remove casserole from heat. Discard bay leaf and parsley sprigs. Using a slotted spoon, transfer vegetables to a serving platter and chicken pieces to a carving board. Remove the bones and skin from the chicken and cut the meat into small slices. Make a shallow well in the center of the vegetables and arrange the chicken slices in the well. Return bones and skin to the liquid in the casserole. Cool the chicken and vegetables, then cover with plastic wrap and refrigerate.

Place the casserole over high heat and bring the liquid to a boil. Reduce to a simmer and cook until the liquid has reduced by one third. Pour the liquid through a strainer into a bowl and discard all the solids in the strainer. Filter the liquid into a clean bowl, passing it through a fine sieve lined with a double layer of moistened cheesecloth. Let it cool, then chill until all the fat rises to the surface. Lift off all the fat, leaving the aspic behind. Pour about ½ cup of the aspic into a saucepan and melt it, then let it cool just to the point of setting.

Remove chicken from the refrigerator. Carefully spoon barely set aspic over the chicken and vegetables. Use a fork to break up the rest of the firm aspic and spoon it around the serving platter. Serve at once.

Béchamel-Based Chaudfroid Sauce

Blade mace imparts a delicate and subtle flavor to this chaudfroid sauce. If you cannot find it, omit the spice altogether. Even the smallest amount of ground mace would be overpowering.

makes about 2½ cups

2	cups milk	1½	envelopes (4½ scant teaspoons) unflavored gelatin
1	blade of mace		
1	bay leaf	6	tablespoons light cream
1	slice of shallot	½	teaspoon salt
6	peppercorns	¼	teaspoon freshly ground white pepper
1	tablespoon butter		
2	tablespoons flour		
6	tablespoons cold water		

Make the béchamel: Pour the milk into a small saucepan; add the mace, bay leaf, slice of shallot and the peppercorns. Set over low heat for 5 to 7 minutes to infuse the milk with the flavors of the herbs and spices. Strain the milk into a bowl and discard the flavorings. Wash and dry the saucepan. Melt the butter over low heat and then add the flour, stirring with a wooden spoon to make a smooth paste. Stirring constantly, gradually pour in the flavored milk. When all the milk has been added, return pan to heat and bring the sauce to a boil, still stirring. Simmer the sauce for 2 minutes. Remove pan from the heat.

Pour the cold water into another small saucepan, sprinkle the gelatin over it, and soak for 5 minutes. Scrape the softened gelatin into the sauce and stir over low heat until the gelatin is completely dissolved and mixed into the sauce. Stir in the cream, salt and pepper. Strain the sauce into a bowl, stirring as it cools. When it is as thick as heavy cream and on the point of setting, it is ready to use.

Chicken in Chaudfroid and Clarified Aspic

Master Recipe for Clarified Aspic and Velouté-Based Chaudfroid Sauce

6 to 8 portions

1	roasting chicken, about 4 pounds	1	teaspoon salt
		2	eggs
1	onion	6	tablespoons cold water
1	carrot	1½	envelopes (4½ scant teaspoons) unflavored gelatin
1	celery rib		
1	Bouquet Garni (see Volume 1 Index)	6	tablespoons heavy cream garnishes of your choice
6	black peppercorns		

Truss the chicken and place in a large pot along with the giblets. Cover with water, bring to a boil, then pour off the water. If there is scum deposited on the sides of the pot, wash it. Return chicken to the pot and cover with fresh water. Peel and quarter the onion. Scrape and halve the carrot; string and halve the celery rib. Add vegetables to the chicken along with the *bouquet garni,* peppercorns and salt. Bring the water to a boil, reduce heat, cover, and simmer gently for 1 to 1½ hours, or until the chicken is tender. Let the bird cool in the liquid for about 30 minutes, then transfer to a platter. Reserve the liquid. When the chicken is completely cool, cover it with wax paper to keep it from drying out and refrigerate it.

Make the aspic: Pour the cooking liquid through a colander into a bowl to remove all the solids, then pour through a fine sieve lined with a double layer of moistened cheesecloth. Let the stock cool completely, then remove any fat that has risen to the surface. Measure 3 cups of the stock into a saucepan. (If there is more, it can be stored for other uses.) Separate the eggs, reserving the yolks for another use. Beat the egg whites until frothy, and crush the eggshells. Add both to the stock and bring it to a boil, whisking constantly. The egg whites and shells will rise to the top, collecting any particles that would cloud the stock. Let the stock remain over very low heat for 30 minutes, then lift off the egg mass and discard it. Ladle the clarified stock through a fine sieve lined with a double layer of moistened cheesecloth into a clean saucepan. Place the cold water in a small bowl and sprinkle the gelatin over it; soak for 5 minutes. Scrape the softened gelatin into the stock and stir over low heat until the gelatin is dissolved and completely combined with the stock. Pour 1 cup of the aspic into a small metal bowl and set aside. Stir occasionally.

Make the chaudfroid: Make velouté sauce with the remaining 2 cups stock (see Volume 3 Index). Let the sauce cool slightly, then stir in the cream and mix well. Set the velouté, which is now ready to be used as chaudfroid, over a container of crushed ice. Stir the chaudfroid from time to time as it cools.

Remove chicken from the refrigerator. Carefully peel off the skin. Remove wing tips with poultry shears or a very sharp knife. To make carving easier, remove the wishbone: Scrape the meat from the bone, free the base at both sides, run your finger up the bone, and twist it away at the top. Rub the flat of a knife gently over the chicken to make the surface completely smooth. Fix the bird on a wire rack with a skewer. When the chaudfroid sauce is on the point of setting, coat the bird with it, doing first one side and then the other (see Technique photos). Arrange the garnishes of your choice on top and chill it for 1½ hours, or until the chaudfroid is set.

Shortly before the chaudfroid is set, put the reserved bowl of aspic—the aspic should be syrupy—in a larger bowl of crushed ice. Stir occasionally until aspic is just on the point of setting. Then glaze the entire surface of the chaudfroid with the clear aspic. Chill again, for at least 1 hour, or until the aspic glaze is set.

Lamb Chops in Mint Aspic

4 portions

2   rib portions of lamb, made
      of 4 rib chops each
      salt and freshly ground
      pepper

1   small bunch of fresh mint
2   cups clarified liquid aspic,
      made from beef stock

Have butcher remove chine bone but ask him not to chop the bones across. Trim the flap from the meat. Peel off the skin and scrape off 1 inch of meat at the end of each chop bone. Preheat oven to 350°F. Place the meat, fat side down, in a roasting pan. Roast for 20 minutes on each side, or until done to your taste. Season with salt and pepper. Set the meat aside to cool.

Wash, dry, and chop the mint. Before the aspic starts to set, add the mint. Cut the cold meat into chops. Place them on a wire rack and coat them with aspic, spooning just enough over them so it runs down the sides. Chill the chops for about 1 hour to set the aspic. Transfer chops to a serving platter.

Molded Parsleyed Ham

6 to 8 portions

2	pounds boned ham, freshly cooked or canned	2	teaspoons unflavored gelatin	
2	bunches of fresh parsley		parsley or watercress for garnish	
4	cups clarified liquid aspic			

Trim freshly cooked ham of any fat or gristle. If using canned ham, drain off any liquid and scrape off any jelly. Cut either ham into 1-inch cubes. Wash and dry the parsley and mince it with a chef's knife or in a food processor fitted with the steel blade. (Stems should be discarded if you are chopping by hand; they can be included if you are using the processor.) Pour the liquid aspic into a saucepan and sprinkle the gelatin on top. Soak for 5 minutes. Heat gently until the softened gelatin is completely dissolved and stir to mix well. Stir the

minced parsley into the aspic. Pour the aspic into a metal bowl, set it over a container of crushed ice, and stir as it cools.

Rinse the inside of a 6-cup mold. Spoon enough aspic into the mold to make a thin layer and let it set. When the aspic in the bowl is on the point of setting, stir in the cubes of ham. Spoon the mixture into the mold, using all of the ham. If there is too much aspic, set it aside for another use. Cover the mold and chill it in the refrigerator for about 3 hours, or until the aspic is firmly set. Turn out the mold on a round platter and garnish with parsley or watercress sprigs.

Jellied Chicken Breasts

4 portions

6	scallions	½	teaspoon salt
1	1-inch piece of fresh gingerroot	¼	teaspoon freshly ground pepper
4	boned and skinned chicken breast halves, each about 8 ounces	4	tablespoons sherry
		¼	cup cold water
4	thin slices of smoked ham	1	envelope (1 scant tablespoon) unflavored gelatin
2½	cups Chicken Stock (see Volume 1 Index) or canned broth		

Trim and chop the scallions. Peel gingerroot and cut into thin slices. Wrap each chicken breast in a slice of ham and place the pieces in a flameproof casserole. Pour in the stock and add the salt, pepper, chopped scallions and sliced gingerroot. Set the casserole over moderate heat and bring the liquid to a boil. Reduce heat to low, cover the casserole, and simmer gently for 45 minutes, until the chicken is tender. With a slotted spoon carefully transfer the chicken breasts to a serving dish.

Strain the cooking liquid into a bowl, then return it to the casserole. Pour in the sherry. Pour the water into a cup,

sprinkle the gelatin on top, and let it soak for 5 minutes. Set the casserole over moderate heat and bring to a simmer. Scrape the softened gelatin into the liquid and stir over low heat until the gelatin is completely dissolved. Remove casserole from the heat and pour the aspic into a metal bowl set over a larger container filled with crushed ice. Stir occasionally, just until aspic is on the point of setting. Spoon it carefully over the chicken pieces to make an even coating. Chill. When the first coat is set, a second coat can be spooned over it. Chill the dish for at least 3 hours, or until the aspic is completely set. Serve directly from the dish.

Chicken Galantine in Chaudfroid

This is a master recipe for a galantine. Be sure to leave yourself plenty of time. Begin preparations in the morning for an evening meal or break the preparations by making the stock the night before.

6 to 8 portions

1	oven-ready chicken, 3½ pounds		large pinch of cayenne pepper
1	slice white bread		large pinch of grated mace
6	ounces boneless veal	4	tablespoons dry sherry
6	ounces boneless lean pork	1	large egg
1	Spanish onion	1½	pounds ripe tomatoes
2	tablespoons drained capers	½	cup dry white wine
6	ounces mushrooms	1	teaspoon unflavored gelatin
2	tablespoons unsalted butter		garnishes: radish slices, cucumber skin and pieces, orange peel and slices, whole cloves
2	tablespoons chopped fresh parsley		
	salt and freshly ground pepper		

Bone the chicken (see Volume 8 Index). Cover lightly and refrigerate until needed. Use the chicken bones and gizzards to make 5 cups stock (see Volume 1 Index). After stock has simmered for 3 hours, make the stuffing. Whirl the bread in a blender or processor to make ½ cup crumbs. Mince the veal

and pork. Peel and mince the onion. Chop the capers. Wipe mushrooms with a damp cloth or paper towels, trim the base of the stems, and chop caps and stems. Melt the butter and sauté the mushrooms until lightly browned. Remove from heat and let mushrooms cool completely. Put the meat and minced onion in a bowl and add the cold mushrooms and any butter remaining in the pan, the bread crumbs, parsley and capers. Season well with salt and pepper and add the cayenne and mace. Pour in the sherry. Beat the egg lightly and add to the bowl. Mix ingredients until well combined. Season and stuff the chicken; roll and wrap it as shown in the Technique photos for Chicken Galantine.

Wash, core, and seed tomatoes, chop them, and put into a pan large enough to hold the galantine. Strain the stock through a colander and then through a fine sieve lined with a double thickness of dampened cheesecloth. Add the white wine. Place the galantine in the pan and pour in enough strained stock to cover it completely. Cover the pan. Simmer the galantine for 1½ hours. Drain the cooked galantine over the pan for a few seconds, then set it aside to cool. Strain the stock again and set it aside.

When the galantine is cool enough to handle, tighten the wrapping or rewrap the galantine, top with a plate and press under a weight. Cool completely at room temperature, then refrigerate until needed. Use 3 cups of the strained stock to make aspic. Test for jelling and if more gelatin is needed pour ½ cup of the aspic into a small saucepan and sprinkle the teaspoon of gelatin on top. (Set the rest of the aspic aside and stir occasionally.) Make 1½ recipes Velouté Sauce (see Volume 3 Index) and bring to a simmer. Dissolve the soft-

ened gelatin mixture in it, stirring to mix well. Set this chaudfroid sauce over crushed ice and stir occasionally until it is thick enough to coat the back of a spoon.

Unwrap the cold galantine and remove the trussing strings. Set the roll on a wire rack over a tray or platter. Coat the roll with the chaudfroid sauce, spooning it along the center and allowing it to run down the sides to cover the galantine completely. Lay the garnishes in the sauce, making an attractive design. Transfer the galantine, still on the rack, to the refrigerator to set for 2 hours.

Shortly before the chaudfroid is set, place the reserved bowl of aspic—the aspic should be syrupy—in a larger bowl of crushed ice. Stir occasionally until aspic is just on the point of setting.

When the chaudfroid coating is firmly set, remove the galantine from the refrigerator and pour the chilled aspic over it. Return the galantine to the refrigerator to set for 2 hours longer.

Place the galantine on a platter large enough for both serving and slicing.

Variation: If you do not have time to apply an aspic coating and let it set, chill the aspic in a large flat pan until it is firm enough to be chopped (see Introduction). Spoon the aspic diamonds around the galantine.

Fish Aspic

makes about 4 cups

1½	pounds fish bones, heads and skins	½	teaspoon dried tarragon
1	onion	1	cup white wine
2	carrots	5	cups water
1	Bouquet Garni (see Volume 1 Index)	2	eggs
6	peppercorns	½	cup cold water
½	teaspoon salt	2	envelopes (2 scant tablespoons) unflavored gelatin

Make a fish stock: Break up the bones and heads and place them and any fish skins in a large saucepan. Peel the onion and scrape the carrots. Cut both into chunks and add to the bones along with the *bouquet garni,* peppercorns, salt and tarragon. Pour in the wine and the 5 cups water. Set the pan over moderate heat and bring the liquid to a boil. Partly cover the pan, reduce heat to low, and simmer the bones for 30 minutes.

Pour the contents of the pan through a strainer into a bowl. Discard bones, vegetables, herbs and spices. Ladle the strained stock through a fine sieve lined with dampened cheesecloth set over an enamelware or stainless-steel saucepan. Do not pour it, as there may be sediment in the bottom of the bowl that would cloud the aspic. Let the stock cool until any particles of fat rise to the surface. Blot these up with paper towels.

Separate the eggs, reserving the yolks for another use. Beat the egg whites with a wire whisk until frothy and crush the shells. Set the pan of stock over moderately high heat,

drop in crushed shells and egg whites, and immediately start whisking the stock, continuing until it comes to a boil. Remove pan from heat until the boiling subsides, then set it over very low heat and maintain it at a bare simmer for 30 minutes. Remove from heat and let it cool for 15 minutes. Lift off the egg-white mass with a skimmer. Ladle the stock through a fine sieve lined with dampened cheesecloth, and, as before, be careful to leave any sediment on the bottom of the pan.

Pour the ½ cup cold water into a saucepan and sprinkle the gelatin over it. After 5 minutes, scrape the softened gelatin into the pan of stock and dissolve it over low heat; make sure it is completely dissolved and that no granules are sticking to the pan. Test for jelling by refrigerating 2 tablespoons of stock; if jelly is not firm, add a little more gelatin, 1 teaspoon at a time, softening and dissolving it as described. Cool the aspic, then chill in the refrigerator until ready to use, or set over crushed ice and stir occasionally until it is on the point of setting and ready to use.

Jellied Veal

Serve this cold dish with a selection of salads for a cold luncheon or buffet.

6 to 8 portions

2	pounds boned leg of veal	¾	cup white wine
8	bacon slices	2½	cups water
1	small onion	6	cooked artichoke bottoms
1	celery rib	1	large cucumber
1	carrot	¼	cup cold water
1	Bouquet Garni (see Volume 1 Index)	1	envelope (1 scant tablespoon) unflavored gelatin
¼	teaspoon salt		
½	teaspoon freshly ground pepper		

Tie the veal into a neat shape if the butcher has not done it and wrap the bacon slices around the veal, securing them

with toothpicks or string. Place the veal in a large saucepan. Peel and slice the onion. Trim, string and chop the celery.

Scrape and chop the carrot. Add the vegetables to the veal along with the *bouquet garni,* salt and pepper. Pour in the wine and the 2½ cups water. Bring the liquids to a boil over high heat. Cover the pan, reduce heat to low, and simmer the veal for 1¼ hours, or until it is very tender when pierced with the point of a knife and its juices run clear. Remove pan from the heat and let the veal cool slightly in the cooking liquid.

Meanwhile, trim the artichoke bottoms and cut them into thin slices. Peel the cucumber, halve it, and scoop out the seeds. Cut the cucumber into ¼-inch slices. Pour the ¼ cup water into a small saucepan and sprinkle the gelatin over it to soak for 5 minutes. With slotted spoons, transfer the cooked veal to a carving board. Strain the cooking liquid into a saucepan and bring to a boil over high heat. Scrape the softened gelatin into the hot liquid, reduce heat to a simmer, and stir until the gelatin has dissolved completely. Set the aspic aside to cool.

Rinse a 6-cup soufflé dish with water. Cut the veal into 1-inch cubes and arrange about one quarter of them on the bottom of the soufflé dish. Arrange a layer of one third of the artichoke slices on top, then place one third of the cucumber slices over the artichokes. Repeat layers until all ingredients are used, ending with a layer of veal cubes. Pour the cooled aspic over the mixture, making sure it runs down to the bottom and fills all the spaces between the meat and vegetables. Chill the dish in the refrigerator for at least 4 hours, or until the aspic is firmly set.

Remove soufflé dish from the refrigerator. Dip the base quickly into hot water. Place a serving dish over the top. Holding the dishes firmly together, turn them over. The jellied veal should slide out easily.

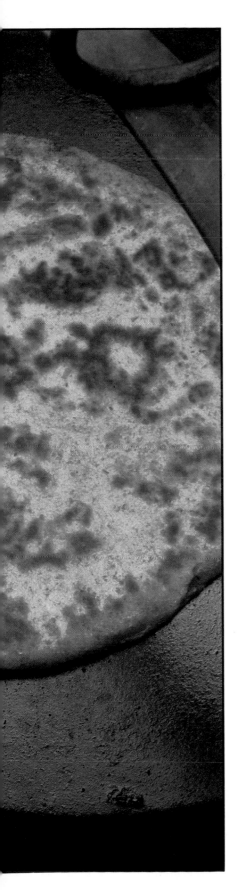

Part Three
FLAT BREADS

If, in its long history, bread reached the pinnacle of its development with, let us say, the French croissant, then the flat bread, though still very much with us today, can be traced to the very dawning of civilization.

Before some form of flat bread came about, things, gastronomically speaking, were rather crude. Troglodyte food gatherers, like their not-so-distant ancestors, the apes, must have occasionally grazed on raw grains, and may even have learned to thresh the grains to make them more palatable. But with the discovery of fire and the subsequent ability to boil water, or at least simmer it, came what in all likelihood was the first gruel or porridge of lightly threshed wild grain. It's easy to imagine how one day some thickened porridge warming in a bladder by the fire accidentally spilled onto one of the hot stones that formed a crude hearth. And there you have it! In one stroke the griddle was invented, and, in its simplest form, the flat bread.

For centuries flat bread would remain *the* bread, though no doubt with refinements of one sort or another, mostly having to do with the varieties of grain that were first gathered, then cultivated, and with techniques that were used for separating the grain from its husk. As the human race spread out and articulated itself into divergent cultures, the varying pace of technological progress, social organization, climatic conditions, and the availability and nature of the foodstuffs all had a profound effect on the methods and style of food preparation and most particularly on the making of bread.

Those peoples who remained nomadic ate in one way; those who built villages, towns and cities ate in another. Ovens, even rudimentary ones, were a luxury reserved for people who led a relatively stable life. Indeed, the technology required to build a house was much the same, at least in the Middle East, as that required to build an oven. People on the move would simply resort to the griddle stone and were unlikely to have the time or means to add leavening to their bread, even if they were familiar with the methods of doing so. The Jews, for instance, in their haste to flee from the Pharaoh, camped for days on end in the desert, where they had little time and few tools with which to cook. They made a simple, flat, unleavened bread called matzo. Matzos are still eaten today for their own delicious sake and also, of course, to commemorate the hardships of the exodus. And though they're rarely made at home anymore, the ingredients remain as simple and pure as ever—flour and water.

In many cultures, another factor crucial to the persistence of flat breads has been the inability to grow wheat. Wheat is the only grain that contains a significant quantity of gluten, the gelatinous substance that gives dough its elastic quality. Without that elasticity, the dough will not catch and trap the gas bubbles that result from the leavening process; therefore, the dough must have at least a portion of wheat flour in it or the baked loaf will remain essentially a flat bread. Thus, for instance, in ancient Greece, where barley was prevalent and wheat almost unknown, raised bread was also unknown until the time of Alexander, when wheat was introduced to the region.

It should be noted that throughout history and in different parts of the world, bread, while remaining everywhere a basic food, served a number of very different functions. For many ancient people bread was neither a sop for gravy nor an accompaniment for other food but a meal in itself. What's more, it was an easily portable meal that might be kept for weeks or longer without spoiling. And, of course, in the absence of modern preservatives, it was the drier, unleavened breads that kept best.

There were, of course, no spoons, per se, in ancient days, and precious few objects that might pass for what we call plates. Inevitably, pieces of flat bread became a means of conveying hot or messy stews or other foods from pot to mouth, much as we tear off pieces of pita bread and dip them in a bowl of *hummus* or *baba ganoush.* In Mexico, fresh tortillas, when they are not simply eaten out of hand, are wrapped around a savory filling to make *enchiladas* and *tacos,* while stale tortillas are usually cut into small pieces, fried in oil until they are crisp and then used to lift dips and spicy sauces. Likewise, crisp Scandinavian flat breads, today as much as in the past, often provide an edible platform for elaborate *smørrebrød* sandwiches.

The term "trencherman," with which we refer to the serious-minded and truly capable eater, derives from the medieval trencher, a hard flat slab of bread or wood that was, in effect, the first dinner plate. At aristocratic tables, meals of highly sauced meats and other food were fished out of the communal serving pot with the fingers, and placed first on the flat-bread trencher before being conveyed, also with the fingers, to the mouth. After the meal, the gravy-soaked trenchers were eaten by the dogs or the servants.

In many places around the world it is still considered not only proper, but more highly cultured, to eat without utensils, using only the fingers and a piece of bread. Most of the Asian breads and many African and Middle Eastern breads—soft, flat and delicious—are torn into small pieces and used to wrap morsels of food and thus to convey them from plate to mouth.

Today, flat breads are rather easier to recognize than to define, partly because they are, after so many centuries, as diverse and varied as the cultures that make them. Some, like the Middle Eastern pita, are leavened; some, like matzos, never are. Some are crisp, hard and crunchy, while others are soft and chewy. Most flat breads are simple breads in the sense that they are made up of the most basic ingredients, but it is this very simplicity that accounts for their age-old popularity. For in the end, who can resist the natural pure flavors of nature's two most basic ingredients—grain and water.

FLAT BREADS

Most flat breads fall into the category of breads that we think of as store-bought rather than homemade, although this is not necessarily because they are difficult to make, but rather because they are so readily available on the supermarket shelves and are by and large the kinds of breads that tend to keep well for extended periods of time.

Making your own flat breads at home is extremely rewarding, however, and requires little in the way of effort and skill. The dough is quickly made and in general the only really time-consuming part of the process is the rolling out and shaping. Cooking times, too, are very short, so that start-to-finish you can usually have fresh homemade bread or crackers in under an hour.

GRIDDLE-BAKED BREADS

Many flat breads are baked on a griddle or in a heavy cast-iron skillet and in some ways these simple breads are the most elemental and satisfying of all. Mexican tortillas and Indian chapatis fall into this category, as do Scottish oat bannocks.

Tortillas

These flat, unleavened pancake-like breads are a staple ingredient of every Mexican and Tex-Mex meal. There are two basic types of tortillas—one made with corn flour (*masa harina*), the other made with wheat flour (*harina de trigo*). Included in this section is a recipe for tortillas made with corn meal (which you should use only in the event that you cannot find corn flour). They will not be as authentic and their texture will not be quite right, but they will still be delicious.

Helpful Hints. The dough for both corn-flour and corn-meal tortillas will not be as elastic as a dough that is made from any kind of wheat flour because corn flour contains almost no gluten. If your dough is too dry and won't hold together, add a little more water until it does.

It is possible to learn to flatten the corn-flour tortillas with the palms of your hands but this takes time and practice. A tortilla press (available in cookware stores and many Mexican groceries) considerably reduces the amount of labor involved in making tortillas.

It is essential to get your heavy cast-iron skillet or griddle *very* hot before baking the tortillas. You should be able to detect a faint blue haze rising from the surface before starting to cook the tortillas.

Tortillas may puff up slightly while they are baking, so it is useful to have a

Asian Unleavened Bread

eight 4-inch rounds

1	cup whole-wheat flour	¼	cup milk
1	teaspoon salt	¼	cup water

4 Turn out onto lightly floured board and knead until smooth and elastic, about 10 minutes.

5 Lightly oil the inside of a plastic bag and place the dough in it. Leave at room temperature for 30 minutes so dough can relax.

spatula in hand to press down lightly till the bubbles disappear.

Tortillas are best served fresh and warm, but they may be made ahead; reheat by wrapping them in aluminum foil and placing them in a 250°F oven for about 10 minutes.

Leftover or stale tortillas may be fried in vegetable oil until crisp and served in place of other chips and crackers with any number of spicy dips and sauces.

Oatmeal Bannocks and Oat Cakes

Bannocks—a kind of traditional Scottish oat cakes—are delicious eaten with plenty of butter and almost any sweet or savory spread. They are wonderful at breakfast, teatime or any other time. But for best results, bannocks should be made as quickly as possible and served immediately, so have your family ready and waiting.

Use medium or fine oatmeal for bannocks and oat cakes or, if absolutely necessary, rolled oats. Do not use instant oatmeal.

Helpful Hints. Keep a supply of flour nearby as you roll out the dough. Dust your hands, rolling pin and work surface frequently with flour to prevent the dough from sticking.

To get your skillet or griddle good and hot before baking the bannocks, set it over medium-high heat for 3 to 4

1 Place flour and salt in a large bowl and mix together with a fork. Make a well in the center.

2 Mix milk and water together and pour half the liquid into the well. Draw the flour into the liquid, using your fingers to press the dough together.

3 Add more liquid gradually—you may not need to use it all—blending with fingertips, until dough leaves sides of bowl and sticks together.

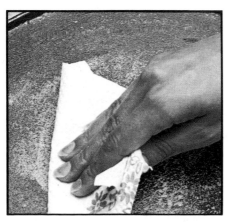

6 Use a well-seasoned cast-iron skillet or griddle or rub skillet or griddle with oil and place over medium heat.

7 Divide the dough into 8 pieces. Roll each piece into a ball, then roll out with a rolling pin into a 4-inch circle.

8 When skillet or griddle is hot, place dough circles on surface. Cook 2 minutes on one side, then turn and cook 2 minutes on the other.

minutes. It is hot enough when you can see a slight haze emanating from the surface.

Chapati

Chapati is the simplest and most basic of the Indian breads. These flat, round, unleavened breads are always made from *atta,* the Indian word for finely ground whole-wheat flour. They are baked on a heavy cast-iron skillet or griddle, and then briefly exposed to an open flame to make them puff and to slightly char the surface.

Chapatis are satisfying earthy breads rich with wheat flavor and of good chewy texture. They are meant to be torn apart with the fingers and wrapped around a morsel of food. They go extremely well with every type of Indian food, but can also be served to great advantage with many Western-style dips, stews and cocktail foods.

Helpful Hints. The dough should be allowed to rest for 30 minutes to 1 hour after it has been kneaded. This allows it to relax and makes it easier to roll out. It can rest for up to 3 hours, kept covered and at room temperature, and for as long as 24 hours, covered and refrigerated.

To prevent the dough from sticking, keep a supply of whole-wheat flour nearby as you roll out the circles of dough and use it frequently to dust your hands, rolling pin and work surface.

Get your skillet or griddle good and hot before baking the breads, at least 3 or 4 minutes over moderately high heat. It is hot enough when you can start to see a slight haze emanating from the surface.

Although chapatis are best served as soon as they are done, if you must hold them you can keep them fresh for up to an hour by buttering each on one side, stacking them, wrapping them tightly with aluminum foil, and keeping them in a 200°F oven.

FRIED BREADS

Flat breads like the Indian pooris, parathas and poppadums have a richer

Cooking Poppadums

1 Pour 2 inches of oil into heavy skillet. When oil is hot, dip poppadum in it, holding poppadum by edge with your fingers or tongs.

2 As soon as the poppadum puffs (about 2 seconds), lift out of the oil. Tap against the edge to shake off excess fat.

taste because they are either lightly sautéed or deep fried in oil.

Poori

The dough for poori is similar to that for chapati, except that oil or butter is added to the flour and water mixture to provide extra richness. Pooris are fried quickly in deep, hot oil, which makes them puff and turn a golden color.

Helpful Hints. Heat the oil to 360°F before adding the first poori. If possible, use a deep-frying thermometer. Check the temperature of the cooking oil from time to time to see if it has dropped below the necessary 360°F.

Fry only one poori at a time. It will drop to the bottom of the frying pan when you first put it in and then almost immediately rise to the surface. Poke the poori down into the hot oil with the back of a slotted spoon so that the hot oil washes over the surface. The poori is done when it puffs like a balloon and turns a rich golden color. Remove it using tongs and a slotted spoon and place on paper towels to drain.

Ideally, pooris should be served immediately; however, they can be held. Stack them, wrap them tightly in aluminum foil, and keep them warm in

a 200°F oven for up to an hour. If you wish to make them a day or so ahead of time, refrigerate them after they are wrapped in foil. To reheat, place the pooris, still wrapped in aluminum foil, in a preheated 350°F oven for about 10 minutes.

Paratha

Paratha is a rich, flaky, layered bread. The dough is repeatedly brushed with clarified butter, folded and rolled. It is then shallow fried in a heavy cast-iron skillet or on a griddle.

Parathas go particularly well with vegetarian cuisine as the rich buttery taste compensates for the absence of meat.

Helpful Hints. As parathas are done, wrap them in aluminum foil and keep them warm in a preheated 200°F oven.

Parathas may be prepared several hours in advance and set aside, covered with a barely damp cloth, until you are ready to fry them. They can also be fried and then reheated either in a frying pan or in a hot oven just before serving.

How to Make Clarified Butter. Clarified butter, or ghee, is used a

 3 Dip uncooked part of poppadum in oil. Cook 2 seconds, then tap against edge to shake off excess fat. Drain on paper towels.

 OR Cook the poppadums in a pre-heated 450°F oven, placing them in a single layer directly on the oven shelf.

great deal in Indian cooking. But it is extremely useful for every other type of cooking as well. The clarifying process removes all the milk solids from the butter and thus permits the butter to be heated to a much higher temperature than regular butter before it burns.

Place unsalted butter in a heavy saucepan or skillet and heat the butter slowly until it melts and becomes frothy. Remove from the heat and carefully skim off all the foam from the top and discard or use as a topping for vegetables. Pour the clear yellow liquid into a heatproof glass jar and discard all the milk solids at the bottom of the pan. Clarified butter keeps extremely well even without refrigeration, but will keep, covered, in the refrigerator for months. Be sure to melt it again if it has been refrigerated.

Poppadums

These paper-thin circles of flat bread are made from legume flour and are the Indian equivalent of potato chips. They can be served all on their own as snacks or as a perfect accompaniment to spicy Indian dishes. Poppadums are almost never made from scratch like other Indian flat breads, but are bought in Asian specialty stores. They come in

two basic varieties—plain or spiced liberally with pungent black pepper. They are quickly fried in very hot oil just before serving time.

Poppadums can also be baked for a few minutes in a very hot oven, but the results are not as crisp and puffy. Uncooked poppadums should be kept tightly wrapped to prevent them from becoming stale and tough.

BAKED BREADS

Some flat breads and crackers (really small flat breads) are oven-baked, as are breads that are leavened and raised, although they are usually in the oven for shorter times and at much higher temperatures.

Pita Bread

The Middle East is the home of many varieties of breads, some flat and others not, some unleavened and others slightly so. But the most famous of them all is undoubtedly pita bread.

Pita is a yeast-raised bread and the dough must have time to rise properly before it is baked. After it has risen, the dough is rolled out into individual rounds, which are then baked in a very hot oven. This hot quick baking causes

the dough to expand and form a closed and hollow pocket. In pita's most well-known presentation—especially in the United States, where the bread is as likely to appear on supermarket shelves as are corn muffins—this pocket is opened and stuffed with filling to make a sandwich.

Helpful Hints. You may wish to review the procedures for working with yeast doughs given in Volume 7.

Pita breads will dry out very quickly unless they are covered and stored in airtight plastic wrap or aluminum foil. Wrapped in aluminum foil, they may be reheated in a 300°F oven for 10 minutes before serving.

Crisp Hard Flat Breads and Crackers

There is an astonishing variety of crisp flat breads in nearly every type of national cuisine. By their very nature, these are breads that keep extremely well over a long period of time. Today they are almost always bought packaged from the supermarket shelves, but the adventurous home cook will find the making of crisp flat breads a very easy and extremely rewarding experience. Crackers, of course, are just small versions of these crisp breads.

Matzo

This famous unleavened Jewish crisp bread is traditionally eaten during Passover. But you can serve it anytime in place of other crackers, and it is especially good with cheeses and all kinds of savory spreads.

Although matzos are usually unsalted and unflavored, they can be sprinkled with coarse salt or poppy seeds before baking.

Lavash

Lavash is an Armenian flat bread that is leavened with a little bit of yeast, and then baked and cooled to a wonderful crisp texture. The crisp round disks are meant to be broken into pieces and eaten with cheese, spreads or any sort of dip.

Corn Meal Tortillas

12 tortillas

2 cups yellow corn meal
½ cup unbleached all-purpose flour

¾ cup water

Combine the corn meal and the flour in a mixing bowl and stir in enough water to make a stiff dough. Remove to a floured board and knead for 5 minutes. Cover with plastic wrap and let rest for 30 minutes.

Divide the dough into 12 balls and use a rolling pin to roll each ball into a thin 6-inch round.

Heat a heavy cast-iron skillet or griddle until very hot and bake tortillas one at a time for 1 minute on each side. Remove baked tortilla to a napkin-lined basket and keep warm while you proceed with the rest.

Corn Flour Tortillas

12 tortillas

2 cups *masa harina* (see note)

1¼ cups warm water

Place the *masa harina* in a mixing bowl and add the water all at once, stirring quickly with a wooden spoon to make a smooth, lump-free dough. Cover bowl with plastic wrap and let the dough rest for 5 minutes.

Place a heavy cast-iron skillet or griddle over medium-high heat to heat up while you shape the tortillas.

Divide the dough into 12 walnut-size balls. Flatten each ball, one at a time, between the palms of your hands. Keep slapping and flattening until you have made a thin round approximately 6 inches in diameter or place between two sheets of plastic in a tortilla press. Close the lid and press just

hard enough to flatten. Open the press and remove the plastic-wrapped tortilla. Carefully peel off one piece of plastic at a time so as not to tear the thin round of dough.

Place one tortilla on the hot skillet and cook for about 1 minute, or until it just begins to dry out around the edges. Flip it with a spatula and cook for 1 minute more. Remove to a napkin-lined basket and keep warm. Repeat the procedure until all tortillas are cooked.

Note: Many supermarkets now carry Quaker brand *masa harina* in the flour section.

Flour Tortillas

18 to 24 tortillas

3½   cups all-purpose flour
2   teaspoons salt

½   cup lard or solid vegetable
     shortening
1   cup warm water

Sift the flour and salt into a mixing bowl. Rub the fat into the flour with your fingertips until the mixture resembles a coarse oatmeal. Pour in the water and mix to make a dough. Knead the dough in the bowl for several minutes and roll into a ball. Cover with plastic wrap and let rest for 1 hour.

Remove the dough to a floured board and knead for a few minutes. Roll the dough into a long sausage and pull off one walnut-size piece at a time. Flatten the piece of dough with your hands and roll it out with a rolling pin to a very thin 6- to 8-inch round.

Heat a heavy cast-iron skillet or griddle until very hot and bake one tortilla at a time for 20 to 30 seconds on each side. Remove to a napkin-lined basket and keep warm while you proceed with the rest.

Poori

(Puff Bread from India)

16 pooris

2   cups whole-wheat flour
1   teaspoon salt
3   tablespoons butter

¾   cup water, approximately
     vegetable oil for deep frying

Follow steps 1 through 5 in Technique photos for basic Asian Unleavened Bread, (pages 58–59), melting the butter and adding it in step 2 together with the water. Eliminate the milk. Remove dough from the plastic bag and knead on a floured board for an additional 2 minutes. Divide the dough into 16 equal portions and roll each into a ball. Dust a rolling pin with flour and roll each ball into a thin round. Place oil to a depth of 2 inches in a heavy deep frying pan and heat to 360°F. Drop in one poori; when it rises to the top, press down with a long-handled slotted spoon and hold for a few seconds. When poori is golden brown, turn it over and fry for a few more seconds until it is puffy, light and browned. Remove with a slotted spoon and drain on paper towels. Serve immediately. You may keep them warm wrapped in aluminum foil in a 200°F oven, but they will not be as crisp.

Variation: Substitute 1 cup unbleached white flour for the same amount of whole wheat for a lighter, more delicate bread.

Chapati

(Indian Whole-Wheat Griddle Bread)

16 chapatis

2 cups whole-wheat flour	1 cup water, approximately
1 teaspoon salt (optional)	

Follow steps 1 through 5 in Technique photos for basic Asian Unleavened Bread (pages 58–59), eliminating the milk. Remove dough from the plastic bag and knead on a floured board for an additional 2 minutes. Divide the dough into 16 equal portions and roll each into a ball. Dust a rolling pin with flour and roll each ball into a thin round. Place a heavy cast-iron skillet or griddle over medium heat for about 3 minutes. It is hot enough when you can detect a slight haze rising from the surface.

Place one chapati at a time on the hot griddle. As soon as bubbles form on the surface (about 30 seconds), turn the chapati with a spatula or tongs. Let the other side cook for 30 seconds. Lift the chapati with tongs and hold it over an open gas flame until it puffs up (if using tongs, be sure to hold them with a potholder during this procedure) or place directly over medium flame of a gas burner for a few seconds. As chapatis are finished, wrap them in aluminum foil and keep warm in a 200°F oven while you finish making the rest. Serve chapatis as soon as all of them are cooked.

Oat Cakes

8 oat cakes

1 cup (4 ounces) medium or fine oatmeal	2 teaspoons sugar
½ teaspoon salt	3 tablespoons water, approximately
½ teaspoon baking powder	2 tablespoons butter

Combine the oatmeal, salt, baking powder and sugar in a mixing bowl. Add 3 tablespoons of water and stir to make a soft dough. If dough is too dry and does not hold together add more water, 1 tablespoon at a time, until it does.

Sprinkle a board with additional oatmeal. Turn dough out on the board and knead lightly for 1 minute, or just until it is smooth. Roll the dough into a circle about ¼ inch thick. With a sharp knife, cut the dough into 8 triangular wedges.

Preheat broiler to hot.

Melt half the butter in a heavy cast iron skillet or griddle set over medium heat. When the foam subsides, add as many oat cakes as will fit comfortably without crowding. Fry them for 5 minutes on one side only, or just until they begin to curl slightly at the edges. Remove oat cakes and keep them warm while you fry the rest in the remaining butter.

When all the oat cakes have been cooked, place them under the broiler, uncooked side up. Broil for 2 minutes, or until they are crisp. Transfer to a serving dish and serve immediately.

Paratha

(Indian Fried Whole-Wheat Bread)

12 parathas

2	cups whole-wheat flour	½	cup clarified butter (see Index)
1	teaspoon salt	¼	cup water, approximately

Sift flour and salt into a mixing bowl. Add 2 tablespoons of melted clarified butter. Rub the butter into the flour with your fingertips until it is all absorbed.

Pour in ¼ cup water and knead the mixture with your hands until it forms a soft dough. If it is too dry, add water, a tablespoon at a time, until the dough is soft and workable.

Turn the dough onto a floured board and knead for 10 minutes, or until it is smooth and pliable. Pat the dough into a ball, cover with plastic wrap or a damp towel, and let it rest for 1 hour.

Divide the dough into 12 equal portions and shape each into a ball. Dust a rolling pin lightly with flour and roll out each ball of dough into a very thin circle.

Brush a circle of dough with clarified butter. Fold it in half to make a semicircle, and then in quarters to make a triangle. Roll it out again, but do not try to make it as large and thin as the first time. Brush it with more clarified butter, repeat the folding process, and roll out carefully once again. Repeat this procedure with all the dough circles.

Brush a heavy cast-iron skillet or griddle with clarified butter and place over medium heat. When it is very hot, add as many parathas as will fit comfortably. Cook for 3 to 4 minutes, or until the underside of each is lightly browned. Brush the tops of the parathas with clarified butter and turn them over with a spatula. Cook for another 2 to 3 minutes, or until parathas are browned all over. Wrap finished parathas in aluminum foil and keep warm in a 200°F oven while you cook the rest.

Pita

8 pitas

1	envelope (1 scant tablespoon) active dry yeast
¼	teaspoon sugar
¼	cup warm water (110° to 115°F)

4	cups unbleached white flour
1	teaspoon salt
1	tablespoon vegetable oil
1	cup water, approximately

Dissolve the yeast and sugar in the ¼ cup warm water and let stand for 10 minutes, until yeast mixture becomes frothy. Sift the flour and salt into a large mixing bowl. Make a well in the center and pour in the yeast mixture and vegetable oil. Draw the flour into the liquid with a wooden spoon, adding more water as necessary until the dough clings together. Turn dough out onto a floured board and knead for 10 minutes, until dough is smooth and elastic. You can also place the dough in the mixing bowl of an electric mixer fitted with a dough hook and knead for 1 to 3 minutes, or until dough is smooth and elastic.

Wash and dry the mixing bowl and coat the inside lightly with vegetable oil. Place the dough in the bowl and turn the dough several times so its surface is coated with oil. This will prevent the dough from drying out. Cover with plastic wrap and set aside for about 2 hours, or until the dough has doubled in size. Punch down the dough, remove it to a floured board, and knead for 1 minute.

Coat two baking sheets lightly with oil. Divide the dough into 8 equal pieces and roll each piece into a ball. Cover with a towel and let rest for 10 minutes. Dust a rolling pin lightly with flour and roll each ball of dough into a circle approximately 4 inches in diameter. Place the pitas on the lightly oiled baking sheets, cover with a towel, and let rise for about 45 minutes, or until they have again doubled in size.

Preheat oven to 450°F. Bake the pitas for 15 minutes, or until they puff and just start to turn brown. Remove from the oven and keep them covered while they are cooling so they don't dry out and turn hard. They will deflate as they cool but there will be a hollow pocket inside when they are cut open.

Oatmeal Bannocks

10 bannocks

½	cup all-purpose flour	1½	cups (6 ounces) medium or fine oatmeal	
2	teaspoons baking powder	⅓	cup milk	
1	teaspoon salt	¼	cup water	
2	tablespoons butter	2	tablespoons vegetable oil	

Sift the flour, baking powder and salt into a mixing bowl. Cut the butter into small pieces, add to dry ingredients, and mix together with a pastry blender or your fingertips until all pieces are pea-size and coated with flour. Continue to work dry ingredients and butter together until mixture has the texture of bread crumbs. Stir in oatmeal with a fork and make a well in the center of the flour mixture. Mix milk and water together and pour into the well. Stir ingredients together to make a soft dough.

Turn the dough out onto a well-floured board and knead it lightly for 1 to 2 minutes, until it holds together well. Dust a rolling pin lightly with flour and roll the dough out into a large circle about ½ inch thick. Using a 3-inch round cookie cutter, cut out 10 circles.

Brush a heavy cast-iron skillet or griddle lightly with oil; if the skillet or griddle is very well seasoned, the oil can be omitted. Set the pan over medium-high heat. When the surface is hot, bake the bannocks, a few at a time, for 8 to 10 minutes on each side. They should rise slightly and turn golden brown.

Remove bannocks to a warmed serving dish. If necessary, brush skillet or griddle with more oil and bake remaining bannocks until all are done. Serve immediately.

Lavash

(Armenian Flat Bread)

four 12-inch breads

4	tablespoons butter	¼	cup warm water (110° to 115°F)
1	envelope (1 scant tablespoon) active dry yeast	4	cups unbleached white flour
		1	teaspoon salt
1	teaspoon sugar	1	cup water, approximately

Melt the butter in a small saucepan and remove from the heat. Dissolve the yeast and sugar in the ¼ cup of warm water and let stand for 10 minutes, until yeast mixture becomes frothy. Sift the flour and salt into a large mixing bowl. Make a well in the center and pour in the yeast mixture and melted butter. Draw the flour into the liquid with a wooden spoon, adding more water as necessary just until the dough clings together. Turn dough out onto a floured board and knead for 10 minutes, until it is smooth and elastic. You can also place the dough in the mixing bowl of an electric mixer fitted with a dough hook and knead for 1 to 3 minutes, or until the dough is smooth and elastic.

Wash and dry the mixing bowl and lightly coat the inside with vegetable oil. Place the dough in the bowl and turn it several times so its surface is coated with oil. Cover with plastic wrap and set aside until the dough has doubled in size, 1½ to 2 hours. Punch down the dough, remove it to a floured board, and knead for 1 minute.

Preheat oven to 450°F. Divide the dough into 4 equal parts and roll each into a ball. Dust a rolling pin lightly with flour and roll each ball of dough into a large rectangle, about 10 × 14 inches, or a large circle, about 12 inches in diameter. Place on unoiled baking sheets and prick all over with the tines of a fork. Bake for 10 to 15 minutes, or until the bottom of the breads begins to brown. Remove from the baking sheets and cool on a rack. If not using immediately, wrap tightly in foil.

Matzo

4 round matzos, 6 to 7 inches in diameter

2	cups whole-wheat flour	corn meal for dusting
1	cup water	baking sheet

Preheat oven to 500°F. Place the flour in a mixing bowl and make a well in the center. Pour in the water and with a wooden spoon draw the flour gradually into the water to make a soft dough. Remove to a well-floured board and knead for 2 minutes. Cut dough into 4 equal parts and roll each portion of dough into a thin circle approximately ⅛ inch thick and 6 to 7 inches in diameter. Pierce each circle all over with the tines of a fork.

If you don't have enough baking sheets to bake all the matzos at one time, roll out only as many circles as you can bake immediately, rolling out the rest as the first ones are done. Place dough circles on a baking sheet that has been lightly dusted with corn meal and bake for 10 minutes. Turn them over and bake for 5 minutes more. The matzos should be brown, crisp, and slightly burnt around the edges. Remove matzos from the oven and cool them on a rack. If not using immediately, wrap them tightly in foil.

Variations: You may replace 1 cup of whole-wheat flour with 1 cup of unbleached white flour, or make them entirely with unbleached white flour. The flavor will be less nutty and intense but they will still be very good. Reduce the water to ¾ cup and add more only as needed to make a soft, workable dough.

Veteken

(Scandinavian Wheat Crackers)

20 crackers

1 cup whole-wheat flour	1 teaspoon ground cumin
4 tablespoons butter	3 tablespoons milk

Preheat oven to 400°F. Coat a large baking sheet with butter. Place the flour in a mixing bowl. Cut the butter into small pieces, add to flour and mix together with a pastry blender or your fingertips until pieces are pea-size and coated with flour. Continue to work dry ingredients and butter together until mixture has the texture of bread crumbs. Stir in cumin with a fork and add the milk, stirring to form a stiff dough. Turn out onto a well-floured board and knead briefly into a smooth ball. Press dough into a rectangular shape and roll out into a thin rectangle. Use a pastry wheel and ruler to divide and cut the dough into 20 equal-size squares. Place on the baking sheet and prick the surface of each cracker with the tines of a fork. Bake for 12 to 15 minutes, or until the crackers are just firm to the touch.

Remove from the oven and allow to cool for 10 minutes. Transfer the crackers carefully to a wire rack to cool completely. Store in an airtight container.

Scandinavian Flat Bread

24 rounds

2½	cups unbleached white flour	8	tablespoons butter
¼	teaspoon salt	1	cup buttermilk
4	tablespoons sugar		

Preheat oven to 400°F. Coat one or two large baking sheets with butter. Sift the flour, salt and sugar into a mixing bowl. Cut the butter into small pieces, add to dry ingredients and mix together with a pastry blender or your fingertips until all pieces are pea-size and coated with flour. Continue to work dry ingredients and butter together until mixture has the texture of bread crumbs. Make a well in the center and pour in the buttermilk. Blend together with a fork until the mixture sticks together. Turn dough out onto well-floured board and knead until it forms a smooth ball. Divide the dough into 4 equal pieces and divide each piece into 6 walnut-size nuggets. Dust a rolling pin lightly with flour and roll each nugget into a very thin circle, 4 to 5 inches in diameter. Place as many dough circles as will fit on the prepared baking sheets and bake for 5 minutes, or until evenly browned. Transfer baked flat bread onto a wire rack to cool. Repeat procedure until all flat breads are baked. If not using immediately, wrap tightly in foil.

Rye Crisp Bread

40 to 50 crisps

1	envelope (1 scant tablespoon) active dry yeast	1	cup rye flour
½	cup warm water (110° to 115°F)	½	cup unbleached white flour
		½	teaspoon salt
		3	tablespoons vegetable oil

Dissolve the yeast in ¼ cup of warm water. Sift both flours and the salt into a mixing bowl. Add the yeast mixture and the vegetable oil to the flour and stir with a wooden spoon. Add the additional ¼ cup water, 1 tablespoon at a time, to make a stiff, sticky dough. Remove to a floured board and leave for 5 minutes. Roll into a ball and place in a lightly oiled bowl. Turn the dough several times to coat it with oil. Cover the bowl with plastic wrap and set aside for 2 to 3 hours. The dough will rise but it will not quite double in volume because of the large quantity of rye flour.

Preheat oven to 375°. Brush two large baking sheets with oil. Remove the dough to a floured board and cut it in half. Keep one half covered while you roll out the other. Roll the dough out into the largest, thinnest rectangle possible and cut it into strips approximately 2 inches wide and 4 inches long. Arrange strips on the baking sheet and bake for 7 to 8 minutes on one side. Turn them over with a spatula and bake an additional 5 minutes, or until they are brown and very crisp. Remove and cool on a wire rack. Continue rolling out, cutting and baking until all are done. Store the rye crisp bread in an airtight container.

Water Crackers

twenty-four 4-inch crackers

⅔	cup unbleached white flour	2	tablespoons butter
¼	teaspoon salt	2	tablespoons water

Preheat oven to 400°F. Coat a large baking sheet with butter. Sift the flour and salt into a bowl. Cut the butter into small pieces, add to dry ingredients, and mix together with a pastry blender or your fingers until all the pieces are pea-size and coated with flour. Continue to work dry ingredients and butter together until mixture has the texture of bread crumbs. Make a well in the center and add the 2 tablespoons water. Blend with a fork until the mixture sticks together. Remove to a well-floured board and knead the dough into a smooth ball.

Roll the dough out with a flour-dusted rolling pin until it is no more than ¼ inch thick. Cut out biscuits with a 2-inch round cookie cutter. (Reroll scraps to make more crackers.) Gently roll each cracker into a thinner, larger circle, approximately 4 inches in diameter.

Arrange crackers on the baking sheet and bake for 8 minutes, until golden and puffy. Remove baking sheet from oven and let crackers rest for 5 minutes. Remove them to a wire rack to cool completely. Store in an airtight container.

Cocktail Crackers

These rich buttery crackers are seasoned with salt and spiked with cayenne pepper, making them an excellent accompaniment to cocktails.

30 to 40 crackers

8	tablespoons unsalted butter, at room temperature	¼	cup nonfat dry milk
		2	teaspoons sugar
½	cup water	2	teaspoons salt
2	cups unbleached white flour	¼	teaspoon cayenne pepper, or to taste

Cut the butter into small pieces and place in a mixing bowl. Heat the water to very warm (around 120°F) and pour it over the butter. Stir in the flour, dry milk, sugar, salt and cayenne pepper. Stir with a wooden spoon to make a soft, almost batterlike dough. Turn out on a floured board and knead for 5 minutes, until dough is smooth and velvety. Roll the dough into a ball and place in a bowl that has been coated with butter. Cover with plastic wrap and let rest for 1 hour.

Preheat oven to 400°F. Turn dough out onto a floured board and divide in half. Keep one half covered while you roll out the other. Roll out into a large rectangle about ⅛ inch thick. Cut into small squares or diamonds with a sharp knife or pastry wheel. Place unbaked crackers on an ungreased baking sheet and pierce each cracker several times with the tines of a fork. Bake for 15 to 20 minutes, or until light brown. Watch carefully toward the end so they do not burn. Remove from the oven and cool on a wire rack. Repeat procedure until all crackers have been baked. Store in an airtight container.

Part Four

PUDDINGS AND CUSTARDS

"The *Pudding* is a Dish very difficult to be describ'd, because of the different Sorts there are of it; Flower, Milk, Eggs, Butter, Sugar, Suet, Marrow, Raisins etc. etc. are the most common Ingredients of a *Pudding.* They bake them in an Oven, they boil them with Meat, they make them fifty several Ways: BLESSED BE HE THAT INVENTED PUDDING for it is a Manna that hits the Palates of all Sorts of People; A Manna, better than that of the Wilderness, because the People are never weary of it. Ah, what an excellent Thing is an *English Pudding! To come in Pudding time,* is as much as to say, to come in the most lucky Moment in the World."

—François Maximilien Misson
(French visitor to England in 1690)
Quoted in *Consuming Passions* by Philippa Pullar

In England—where the pudding reached its apotheosis—the term is used to refer to any sweet course or dessert, be it what we call pudding or anything else from cake to ice cream. The English are a notoriously sweet-toothed nation, and "What's for pudding?" means nothing more specific than "What's for dessert?" In America, on the other hand, the word "pudding" conjures up an image of a sweet, soft-textured, milk-based dessert, perhaps chocolate pudding, tapioca pudding, or rice pudding. The term has a long and complicated history, and a slightly confusing one.

The fact is that "pudding" has referred over the centuries to a bewildering number of dishes, both sweet and savory. Many texts suggest an etymological connection with boudin, a French sausage that combines meat, blood, and cereal. The notion is plausible since the earliest puddings from Greek and Roman times were similar affairs and almost always put into sausage-type casings for steaming. Gradually the casings were replaced with cloth pudding bags for steaming or boiling, and finally, with the advent of ovens in the home, even the pudding bags were put aside.

Another etymological connection is with the Old English word for swelling, and in this we discover one of the more consistent elements of a pudding since, however various they are, all are cooked mixtures that contain starch in one form or another. Perhaps it is the thickening or swelling action of the starch that makes a pudding a pudding.

In any case, there has been with puddings, as with all things culinary, a general historical trend toward refinement with regard to technique as well as ingredients. The English mania for puddings in particular can be traced at least in part to the Norman invasion that brought the French sensibility to bear on peasant dishes that had remained more or less intact since Roman times. The court chefs created pudding masterpieces incorporating the most rarified and expensive of ingredients. And since the demands of the elite dictate fashion and stimulate trade, in the long run the common Saxon folk got back their puddings, and much improved, too. The simple, sweetened porridges of the rustic gave way to flummeries, trifles, and other sublimities. For instance, homey and comfortable rice pudding was combined with vanilla custard (*crème anglaise*) and further enriched with crystallized fruits, heavy cream and brandy to become *riz à l'impératrice,* or rice for an empress, specifically the capricious wife of Napoleon III.

Custard, in its simplest form, is no more than sweetened eggs and cream, or eggs and milk. Heated gently, just to the point of thickening, it is basically a sauce, often served with stewed fruits or puddings. Baked or coddled to the point of setting, it becomes a pudding in its own right, though lacking any starch. Taken to its height, it is crowned with a crust of crackling caramelized sugar and called *crème brûlée,* a wickedly rich concoction that despite its French name appears to be a traditional old English dish said to have been first served in the mid-nineteenth century at Trinity College, Cambridge, where it was called burnt cream. In fact, however, it appears long before that in an English cookbook of 1769 and it, too, may have been the product of the intertwining of French and English cooking.

The Greeks are thought to have invented custard, and, of course, the Romans were quick to adopt the idea, since they had a ready domestic supply of eggs and milk. In medieval kitchens, custards were baked in small pastry cases called *croustades,* and it is often assumed that it is from these that custard got its name.

Custards and puddings, taken together, have been the objects of much culinary experimentation, not only in England, where they stand out as shining exceptions in an otherwise ordinary cuisine, but in France, Italy, Portugal and Spain, not to mention the hundreds of other countries that have their own sweet variations.

PUDDINGS AND CUSTARDS

True puddings are moist mixtures that may be cooked or stirred on top of the stove, baked in the oven, or steamed. There are batter puddings, made from flour; puddings made with some kind of cereal grain (rice, tapioca, semolina, corn, cracked wheat); puddings thickened with starch (cornstarch, arrowroot, flour); cold puddings made firm with gelatin or mousse ingredients, such as beaten egg whites and whipped heavy cream; and custards, made with eggs. Many elegant desserts combine several of these ingredients; for example, peach condé uses rice eggs; chocolate cream uses eggs, flour and gelatin.

Batter Puddings

Batter puddings are generally made from all-purpose flour, salt, sugar, eggs or egg whites and liquid. For a pudding made with 1 cup milk, you will need about ⅔ cup flour, a pinch of salt, 4 tablespoons superfine sugar and 1 egg. There is room for experiment with the formula; the milk may be half milk

Steamed Batter Puddings

1 Prepare a double boiler. Use a steamer over a pan of hot water or set a trivet in the pan and place the pudding dish on it.

2 Coat the pudding dish with 1 tablespoon butter. If using, place fruit or jam in the bottom. This will make a topping when unmolded.

3 Make the batter and pour it onto the topping in the dish, leaving 2 inches of space for the batter to rise.

4 Cover pudding with a sheet of pleated oiled foil. Steam for length of time specified in individual recipe.

5 Rest the pudding for 2 minutes. Run a knife around the edge of the dish, then turn out the pudding on a serving plate.

6 Alternatively, use dariole molds for individual puddings. Cover and steam in water bath in the oven for the length of time specified in the recipe.

Baked Puddings with Rice or Tapioca

1 Scald the milk. Add flavorings and infuse for 20 minutes.

2 If you have used a vanilla bean or citrus peel, remove it. Dry vanilla bean to use again.

5 Preheat oven to 300°F. Dot the surface of the pudding with butter. Sprinkle with cinnamon, nutmeg, nuts or glacé fruits.

6 If you want the pudding to have a skin, place the dish uncovered on a rack in the middle level of the oven.

7 Bake for 2½ to 3 hours, or until the pudding is thick and creamy with a golden skin on top. Serve immediately.

10 A pudding without skin can have fresh fruit or fruit juice stirred in after cooking.

11 For caramel topping, allow pudding to become cold. Sprinkle surface with a thick layer of sugar.

12 Place under a hot broiler until sugar is golden and bubbling. Leave for 5 minutes to set.

3 Butter the baking dish.

4 Place grain in the baking dish. Sweeten milk, stir, and pour over grain. Add dried fruit if used. Soak for 3 hours.

OR Place a layer of fruit or jam in the bottom of the dish. Soak grain separately for up to 3 hours.

OR For a pudding without skin, cover with oiled foil before placing in the oven. Bake for 2½ to 3 hours.

8 To enrich a pudding without skin, cool it for 10 minutes. Beat 2 large egg yolks.

9 Stir eggs into pudding and return pudding to the oven for about 5 minutes to cook the eggs.

13 For a jam topping, dot a thin layer of jam over the pudding before serving.

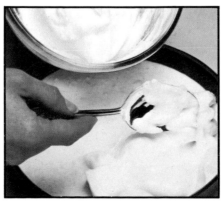

14 For hot meringue topping, cover pudding with meringue. Bake in a 400°F oven for 7 to 9 minutes.

15 For cold meringue topping, make a crisp meringue by baking in a 225°F oven for 30 minutes. Cool.

and half water, or half milk and half light cream, half-and-half, or evaporated milk mixed with water. The batter can be flavored with cinnamon, allspice, cloves or ginger; use 1 teaspoon ground spice for each cup of batter. The spices are especially good if the pudding contains fruit, either fresh or dried.

For baking a batter pudding, use a metal pan for better heat conduction. The pan should be coated with clarified butter (see pages 60–61). For steaming a batter pudding, use a heatproof bowl and set it on a trivet in a steamer or large saucepan.

Pour the clarified butter into the pan and place in a preheated 400°F oven. While the pan and butter heat for 8 to 10 minutes, make the batter. Sift flour and salt into a large bowl and stir in the sugar and any dry flavoring. Make a well in the center and crack the egg into it and add part of the milk. Beat egg and milk with a whisk—beating with the whisk provides max-

imum aeration, more than with either blender or food processor—then slowly bring in the flour and continue whisking until smooth. Add remaining liquid, about 2 tablespoons at a time, and beat until the batter is free of lumps and has the consistency of cream. If you are using moist flavorings, add them at this point. Whisk about 4 minutes longer. The batter should be used immediately, but if you let it stand, be sure to beat it again to restore the aeration.

Bake batter puddings at 400°F.

Simmered Puddings with Semolina or Ground Rice

1 Infuse any flavoring in the milk as for oven-baked puddings.

2 Coat either a heavy saucepan or the top pan of a double boiler with butter.

3 Pour the flavored milk into the saucepan or double boiler top and bring to a simmer.

OR If using large grains, stir occasionally for about 1¾ hours, until the pudding is thick and creamy.

7 If adding eggs, cool the pudding for about 10 minutes. Separate the eggs. Beat the yolks.

8 Stir beaten egg yolks into the pudding. Return pan to heat and simmer for 3 minutes longer.

Allow 40 minutes for a large pudding and 15 minutes for small puddings baked in individual pans. Serve as soon as done; because the only leavening is the air you have beaten into the batter, these puddings tend to deflate quickly.

Puddings Made with Grains

Most grain puddings use milk or cream as the liquid; rice—found in countless different preparations—is the most commonly used grain. When a small amount of rice is used with a lot of liquid, the resulting texture is that of a thick soup, but with different proportions a rice pudding can be firm enough to be molded. While any kind of rice can be used, the best for pudding is a natural rice—short-grain, long-grain or round-grain. Do not use processed rice of any kind. Short grain rice gives a particularly creamy texture and white rice the snowiest appearance.

Ground rice, with a texture like the finest cracked wheat, is also good for pudding; it gives a close-textured mixture that can be molded. If you can't find it pre-ground, prepare it yourself by grinding whole rice in a blender or food processor.

Tapioca is a starch made from the dried roots of the cassava (or manioc) plant. It is a very digestible starch. Puddings made with tapioca are too soft-textured to be molded.

Semolina is made from hard

4 Sprinkle the grain on the surface of the milk, stirring all the time. Stir in sweetening.

5 Bring the mixture to a simmer, stirring all the time. Add dried fruit if used. Reduce heat.

6 If using small grains, stir constantly for 25 to 35 minutes, until the pudding is thickened.

9 If using butter to enrich the pudding, stir it in at this point. Stir until butter is melted.

10 If using fresh fruit or fruit juice, this may be stirred into the pudding at this point.

11 If molding the pudding, whisk egg whites until stiff and fold these into the pudding. Cook as in step 8.

wheat that has been crushed and steamed. It is sold in both fine and medium grades. It is available as couscous in specialty stores and as semolina, farina or Cream of Wheat wherever cereals are sold.

For hot puddings using large grains such as whole rice or tapioca, allow ⅓ cup grain for 2 cups liquid; for cold puddings, add another tablespoon of grain. For hot puddings using small grains (ground rice, semolina), allow about ¼ cup grain for 2 cups liquid; for cold molded puddings, use ⅓ cup grain. The small grains cling together more than the large grains and become very thick. The amounts may seem small, but the grains swell in the liquid. However, some recipes use more grain for a stiffer texture.

A pudding made with 2 cups milk will generally make 4 portions. Use regular whole milk, half milk and half light cream, half-and-half or diluted evaporated or condensed milk. Remember to adjust the sugar if you use either evaporated or condensed milk.

Use granulated or superfine sugar, allowing from 3 to 6 tablespoons for 2 cups milk. Reduce the amount of sugar if the pudding contains dried or candied fruits, as these are naturally high in sugar.

Eggs can be added to bind a mixture. Use 1 large egg for 2 cups milk, or 2 eggs if you are making a molded pudding.

Flavoring a Pudding. The best way to flavor a pudding is to infuse the flavoring ingredients in the milk. For a 4-cup pudding, use a 1-inch piece of vanilla bean and add it to the milk before it is scalded. For a larger pudding use a larger piece of vanilla bean. You may use vanilla extract instead of the bean, but add it later. Vanilla sugar—sugar that has been stored with a vanilla bean in it—can be used to add a delicate vanilla flavor as well, of course, as the necessary sweetening.

Orange or lemon rind can be infused in the same way as the vanilla bean. Orange-flower water or rose water (available in specialty shops and many supermarkets) can be added toward the end of cooking. Use 2 table-spoons for 2 cups milk, or follow the specific recipe directions.

Sweet spices can be added to the milk, or can be sprinkled over a baked pudding just before it goes into the oven. A fortified wine or liqueur, 1½ tablespoons for 2 cups milk, can be stirred into the milk after scalding.

Grated chocolate, 3 ounces for 2 cups milk, is a favorite with children. You may want to adjust the amount of sugar in a chocolate-flavored recipe to your taste. Use orange-juice concentrate, about 1 tablespoon, with chocolate-flavored puddings for delicious results.

Fruit juices or purées can be substituted for part of the milk in a fruit-flavored pudding. Use ½ cup juice to replace an equal amount of milk and stir it in after the grain has been cooked. Use puréed raspberries, strawberries, blueberries, currants, blackberries, peaches, plums, nectarines or oranges. The syrup from preserved ginger or rose hips adds good flavor; use about 2 tablespoons.

Additions and Toppings to Puddings. Dried fruits—currants, dark or light raisins, apricots, pears—or glacé fruits are good additions. Use about 2 tablespoons for 2 cups milk. Chop the larger fruits. There is no need to macerate the dried fruit as they can be soaked with the grain.

Cooked fresh fruits can be layered in the bottom of a pudding dish or stirred into the mixture before molding it or serving it. Juicy fruits and most berries should be stirred in after cooking, but stewed apples, apricots, pears, rhubarb and black currants can be added before. You will need 5 to 6 tablespoons of fruit for 2 cups milk.

Ground almonds add flavor and thickening to a molded pudding; add 3 ounces to 2 cups milk at the end of cooking. Whole hazelnuts make an interesting addition to the pudding and can be cooked in it.

Jam and marmalade can be used to coat the pudding dish, or as a thin filling between layers of a grain dish, or to glaze the pudding when it has finished cooking or as a sauce. If using as a glaze or sauce, warm the preserve and strain it before spooning it over the pudding.

Chopped glacé fruits or sugared nuts can be used as a topping for hot puddings; caramel or grated chocolate is good on cool puddings. Use about 5 tablespoons of fruits, nuts or chocolate for 4 portions.

Preparing a Baked Pudding

This method is particularly good for whole rice and tapioca, because they are improved by slow cooking.

Add flavoring to the milk, scald the milk, and let the flavorings infuse for at least 20 minutes. If you've used vanilla bean or citrus peel, remove it. To make a creamy pudding, soak the grain in the scalded milk, in which the sugar has been dissolved. Soak the grain for at least 1 hour. If you are using dried fruit, soak it along with the grain to plump and soften it. Butter the baking dish and add any jam or fruit to it, then spoon the milk and grain into it. Dot the surface of the pudding with butter and sprinkle with cinnamon or nutmeg.

If you want a pudding with a golden skin, bake uncovered in a 300°F oven for 2½ to 3 hours. If you do not want a skin, cover the dish with oiled foil before baking. Fruit or any other addition can be stirred into the covered pudding after baking and before serving.

Preparing a Simmered Pudding

This method is particularly good for ground rice and semolina.

Butter a saucepan or the top pan of a double boiler. Set the top pan of the double boiler over the bottom with just enough hot water so the top pan does not touch the water. Flavor the milk. Sprinkle the grain on the milk, stirring all the time. Stir in the sugar and any flavoring that has not infused in the milk. Bring the mixture to a simmer. For ground rice or semolina, cook, stirring constantly, for 25 to 35 minutes. Stir occasionally for whole rice and tapioca, allowing 45 minutes to 1½ hours. At the end of the cooking time the grain will be tender and the pudding thick. Stir in any butter or fresh fruit. If eggs are used in the recipe, cool the pudding for 10 minutes before adding them. (When eggs are added to a hot mixture, they cook and set in threads rather than mixing in with the other ingredients.) Separate the eggs. Beat the yolks and stir them into the slightly cooled pudding. Simmer the pudding gently for 3 to 5 minutes long-

er, or until the eggs are cooked and the pudding has thickened. Fresh fruit or juice may be stirred in at this stage. The recipe may direct you to beat the egg whites and fold them in as well. (If not, the egg whites may be used to make a meringue topping.) Spoon or pour the pudding into a serving bowl.

If the pudding is to be molded, coat the mold with oil and place any topping in the base. Pour the pudding into the mold, cover, and chill for 4 hours, or until set. To unmold, first loosen the pudding from the edge of

the mold with a thin sharp knife blade. Invert a serving plate on the mold. Holding the plate and mold firmly together, turn them over. Give them a gentle but sharp downward jerk and lift the mold off.

Preparing a Steamed Pudding

Puddings can be steamed on top of the stove or in the oven, but in either case the steamer, or the saucepan or baking dish you have adapted as a steamer, should be filled with enough water to

Molding a Pudding

1 Make the pudding by the simmering method. Brush a mold with flavorless oil.

2 If mixing fresh fruit or fruit juice with the pudding, add now. Fruit pieces should be small.

3 If using a caramel or fruit topping, place either in the base of the prepared mold.

4 Cool the pudding slightly. Add egg yolks and egg whites as described for simmering method.

5 Pour the pudding carefully into the mold, scraping the pan clean with a rubber spatula.

6 Chill in the refrigerator to set for 2 to 3 hours. Invert a plate over the mold and turn out the pudding.

come halfway up the sides of the mold and the water should be kept at a steady boil during the entire process. Put the pudding dish on a trivet so it does not touch the bottom of the steamer.

Butter the pudding dish and place any fruit or jam in the bottom. Pour in the batter, leaving about 2 inches of space below the rim of the pudding dish to allow room for rising. Cover the dish with oiled foil, pleated in the center to allow for further expansion. Arrange a sling of folded, heavy-duty foil under the pudding dish to simplify lifting it out after steaming. Steam a large pudding for 1 to 1¼ hours, or for the time specified in the recipe. Unmold; cut a large round pudding into wedges, a square pudding into slices or squares. Serve with jam, syrup, custard, brandy or hard sauce.

To fill individual dariole or other small molds, leave 1 inch space for rising, cover in the same fashion, and steam for 40 minutes.

Preparing a Molded Pudding

A molded pudding can be made from almost any type of pudding recipe, but it must be thickened and enriched with whole eggs or whipped cream and possibly also beaten egg whites. Or

Peach Melba Condé

A condé is a rich rice dessert. This is one of several standard methods for making it. You may layer the rice and fruit instead of mixing them together. You may decorate the top with fruit, as we have done here, but if you prefer, you may pour a fruit sauce or jam over the top for contrast of flavors.

6 portions

½	cup milk
½	cup light cream
1	1-inch piece of vanilla bean
4	tablespoons superfine sugar
½	cup round-grain rice, such as Arborio
4	large eggs

1	can (28 ounces) sliced peaches, or 6 fresh peaches, poached and sliced
1½	envelopes (4½ scant teaspoons) unflavored gelatin
½	cup heavy cream
2	tablespoons confectioners' sugar
8	ounces fresh raspberries

1 Place the milk, light cream and vanilla bean in pan. Scald. Leave milk to cool.

5 Drain peaches. Soak gelatin 5 minutes in 6 tablespoons cold water, then dissolve over low heat. Stir into rice with half of the peaches.

6 Chill until pudding is just setting. Whip heavy cream and fold in. Whip egg whites until stiff and fold in.

7 Lightly oil a 5-cup mold. Turn the mixture into the mold and leave to set for 2 to 3 hours.

cornstarch and gelatin can be added if it is to be served cold.

Fruit is used in various ways in molded puddings. It may be layered, used on the bottom, stirred in, or spooned over the top. It must be poached and halved or sliced, although fresh small fruits such as strawberries and raspberries can be used whole and uncooked. You will need 8 ounces of fruit for mixing into a 4-cup pudding, or 1 pound if it is to be used for decoration as well. Dried fruits, soaked in brandy or plain, glacé fruits and crystallized fruits can also be used. To flavor a cornstarch and gelatin pudding, you may use 1 cup of cooked or raw fruit other than citrus fruit.

Caramel may be placed in the bottom of the mold or poured around the unmolded pudding. Toasted nuts can be used for decoration.

The usual flavorings can be used; pudding recipes from the Middle East and India often use orange-flower water or rose water. Extracts and liqueurs can also be added.

If you are making a grain pudding, use whole rice, ground rice or semolina. Tapioca is not good for molding. Add the number of egg yolks called for in the recipe; remember to let the mixture cool before adding the yolks. Whipped cream may be folded in; you will need ½ cup whipped cream for each 1 cup of the basic mixture.

2 Remove vanilla bean and dry it. Stir sugar into milk-cream mixture. Prepare a double boiler and set it over moderate heat.

3 Pour the milk and cream into the top pan of the double boiler. Sprinkle in the rice. Stir over simmering water until thickened.

4 Cool the mixture. Separate 2 eggs and reserve the whites. Beat whole eggs and extra yolks into the rice.

8 Sift confectioners' sugar. Purée the raspberries. Mix sugar with purée to make the Melba sauce.

9 Unmold the pudding on a serving dish. Arrange reserved peaches on top and around the base.

10 Pour Melba sauce over the pudding so it just runs down the sides. Serve remaining sauce separately.

Fold the cream in after the eggs, when the mixture is almost cold. A few special recipes such as *riz à l'impératrice* use custard sauce.

For rice or tapioca mixtures, always use a plain mold. Lumpy mixtures look messy in fancy molds and can be difficult to turn out. Ground rice and semolina can be set in fancy molds. Such a mold should always be oiled. Use almond oil or a flavorless cooking oil. Allow about 2 hours in the refrigerator for the molded mixture to set, or follow specific directions in the recipe.

If you are making a cornstarch and gelatin mixture, use 2 tablespoons cornstarch and 4 tablespoons sugar for 2 cups milk. To set this amount you will need 1 envelope (1 scant tablespoon) unflavored gelatin. Use any kind of mold and brush it with oil. If the mixture has chunks of fruit, a plain mold is preferable. Allow about 2 hours in the refrigerator for setting.

Custard

A custard is a mixture of eggs with various liquids, often milk or cream. Dessert custards are usually sweetened with sugar or honey, but if a fruit purée is used it may provide enough sweetening on its own.

The thickness of a custard depends on the proportion of eggs and liquid. When the custard is thin, it may be served as a sauce. When it is thick, it may be used as a dessert on its own or as the basis for other desserts.

For a thin custard, use 1 whole egg or 2 egg yolks for 1 cup milk; for thick custard use 2 whole eggs or 4 egg yolks, or 1 whole egg and 2 yolks, for 1 cup milk. Use grade AA or A large eggs for the best flavor and the greatest volume. Egg yolks alone give the creamiest color and richest flavor to custards, but whole eggs make a custard set firmer, and therefore are essential for molded custards.

Beginners will find cornstarch a help in stabilizing stirred custards. Cornstarch also helps to prevent curdling of the eggs. Use 1 teaspoon cornstarch for 1¼ cups milk.

The liquid may be whole milk or cream, or a mixture of milk and cream. The richer the liquid, the richer the dish.

Superfine sugar is best for even dissolving. Allow 1 tablespoon sugar to 1 cup liquid. Avoid using too much sugar as it gives a spongy texture to the custard.

Beat the eggs and sugar together with a whisk or rotary or electric beater, particularly important for a mixture that contains whole eggs because it helps to incorporate the whites into the yolks. Scald the milk or cream by pouring it into a heavy saucepan and setting it over moderate heat just until there are bubbles all around the edge; do not let it boil. Remove from heat at once.

Pour the hot liquid gradually into the egg mixture, stirring slowly and constantly with a wooden spoon. Do not beat or you will create air bubbles that will spoil the texture of the finished custard. Strain the mixture into a clean bowl, ideally one with a pouring spout, and pour it into the baking dishes.

Vanilla is the classic flavoring for custards. Use it in the same way as for puddings. Grated citrus peels can be used, as well as liqueurs, melted chocolate, coffee essence and caramel.

Stirred Custard

These custards are prepared over hot water on top of the stove, and stirred constantly with a wooden spoon as they cook. Usually only egg yolks are used, in the proportion of 2 yolks to 1 cup liquid, or 4 yolks to 2½ cups liquid.

You will need a double boiler; be sure the top pan does not touch the water in the bottom. The direct heat of the water, rather than the steam, can cause the eggs to curdle. The water in the lower pan should be gently simmering. The mixture is ready when it coats the wooden spoon. Lift out the spoon and hold it rounded side up. With your finger draw a line across the spoon. If the custard retains the mark made by your finger, it is ready. (If you are using vanilla extract, rather than the whole bean, add it at this point.)

If a stirred custard begins to curdle, proceed as you would for a hollandaise. Plunge the top pan into cold water and stir rapidly with the wooden spoon to speed cooling. Strain the custard through a fine sieve. If the custard actually scrambles, discard it and start again.

Baked Custard

Baked custards frequently use whole eggs as well as egg yolks. Use 2 whole eggs plus 2 egg yolks for 2½ cups milk or other liquid. Scalded milk or cream is poured onto the beaten eggs as in making stirred custard; then the mixture is poured through a fine sieve into the mold or molds. These can be straight-sided metal molds, ring molds, soufflé dishes, or individual soufflé dishes, custard cups, darioles, ramekins or cocottes. The mold is covered with foil and set in a baking pan or other large container. Boiling water is poured into the pan to reach halfway up the sides of the mold. The oven temperature must be just right, for custards need gentle heat; they are poached rather than steamed. The usual temperature is 300° or 325°F.

Bake a custard made with 2½ cups milk for 30 to 40 minutes, or for the time given in a specific recipe. Test by inserting the tip of a knife blade; if it makes a visible mark, the custard is cooked. If the custard flows together again, it is not cooked. Do not leave a cooked custard in the oven; remove it immediately from the oven and the water bath. The heat of the turned-off oven and the heat retained in the water bath or the dish—even one so small as a dariole—causes the custard to continue to cook so the dish must be set out to cool at once.

Baked custards are often served in the baking dishes, but they can be turned out and they are then called *crème renversée*.

Cool a custard that is to be served cold at room temperature before chilling or it may separate. When cooled to room temperature, cover the custard again with foil or plastic wrap, and chill it in the refrigerator. Do not attempt to unmold a custard until it has chilled for several hours.

Steamed Chocolate Pudding

4 portions

8	tablespoons plus 2 teaspoons butter	2	tablespoons brewed strong black coffee
4	ounces semisweet cooking chocolate	⅝	cup superfine sugar
		5	large eggs
		⅔	cup chopped walnuts

Coat a 4-cup pudding dish with 1 teaspoon of the butter. Coat a large sheet of foil with another teaspoon of butter. Break the chocolate into small pieces and place in a heavy saucepan. Pour in the coffee. Set the pan over low heat and melt the chocolate in the coffee, stirring frequently. Remove pan from the heat and cool the mixture. Meanwhile, cream the 8 tablespoons of butter and the sugar together with a wooden spoon until light and fluffy. Separate the eggs. Beat the yolks, one at a time, into the butter mixture, then gradually stir in the melted chocolate. Add the chopped walnuts and beat until all the ingredients are thoroughly combined. Beat the egg whites to stiff peaks. With a metal spoon or rubber spatula, fold egg whites into the chocolate mixture until well blended. Spoon the mixture into the prepared pudding dish.

Pleat the foil and tie it, with the buttered side next to the pudding, over the top of the pudding. Place the dish on a trivet in a saucepan or place it in a steamer and pour in enough boiling water to reach halfway up the sides of the dish. Cover the saucepan and set it over low heat. Steam the pudding for 1 to 1¼ hours, or until a knife inserted halfway between the center and the edge comes out clean. Remove pudding from the water bath, discard paper and foil, and serve immediately.

Orange Custard

6 to 8 portions

2½	cups light cream	5	egg yolks
2	sugar cubes	½	cup granulated sugar
1	orange	2	tablespoons brandy

Preheat oven to 325°F. Scald the cream by heating it until bubbles appear at the edge of the pan. Rub the sugar cubes all over the rind of the orange until they have absorbed the oil. Put the sugar cubes in a mixing bowl and crush them with the back of a wooden spoon. Add the egg yolks and the granulated sugar to the crushed sugar cubes and mix well with the wooden spoon. Squeeze the orange and add the juice along with the brandy. Gradually stir in the scalded cream. Strain the mixture into 6 individual custard pots. Cover the pots with lids or aluminum foil and set them in a deep baking pan. Add enough boiling water to come halfway up the sides of the pots. Bake the custards on a rack in the lower part of the oven for 30 minutes, or until a knife inserted in the center comes out clean. Remove custard pots from the oven. The custard may be served hot or cold.

Port and Raspberry Kissel

A kissel is a traditional Russian fruit pudding.

4 to 6 portions

1	pound fresh raspberries, or 1½ packages (15 ounces) frozen raspberries, without syrup	¾	cup port wine
		½	cup sugar
		1	orange
		2	tablespoons arrowroot
		1¼	cups boiling water

Hull the raspberries and wash them quickly and gently. Turn them onto a layer of paper towels to dry. Place berries and port in a saucepan over high heat and bring to a boil, stirring constantly. Reduce heat to low and simmer for 15 minutes, until raspberries are beginning to be reduced to a purée. Remove pan from the heat and place fruit in a fine wire strainer set over a mixing bowl. Using the back of a wooden spoon, rub the berries through the strainer until only the seeds are left. Discard the seeds. Return the purée to the saucepan and stir in the sugar. Bring to a boil over moderate heat, stirring constantly. Remove pan from the heat and set it aside.

Grate the orange rind to measure 2 teaspoons. Dissolve the arrowroot in ¼ cup cold water in a mixing bowl. Gradually add the 1¼ cups of boiling water, stirring constantly until the liquid thickens. Stir the mixture into the raspberry purée and add the orange rind. Return pan to the heat and cook the mixture, stirring constantly, until it is thick and smooth. Pour the mixture into a serving dish and serve immediately, or chill.

Lemon Tapioca Pudding

4 portions

2	lemons	½	teaspoon ground allspice
⅓	cup uncooked pearl tapioca	4	teaspoons butter
2	tablespoons superfine sugar	3	eggs
1	cup milk	2	tablespoons light brown sugar
1¼	cups light cream		

Set the tapioca to soak in water to cover for 1 hour. Grate the rind from the lemons and squeeze enough juice to measure 2 tablespoons. Place the tapioca, superfine sugar, lemon rind, milk and cream in a saucepan. Set the pan over moderately low heat and cook the mixture, stirring frequently, for 15 minutes, until it is fairly thick. Remove pan from the heat. Stir in the lemon juice and the allspice. Set aside to cool to lukewarm.

Preheat oven to 350°F. Use 1 teaspoon of the butter to coat a deep 4-cup baking dish. Separate the eggs. Beat the egg yolks into the cool tapioca mixture. Beat the egg whites until they form stiff peaks. With a metal spoon or rubber spatula, fold the egg whites into the tapioca mixture. Spoon the pudding into the prepared baking dish. Sprinkle the brown sugar on top. Cut remaining 3 teaspoons butter into small bits and dot them over the sugar. Place the dish in the center of the oven and bake the pudding for 25 to 30 minutes, or until it is thick and creamy and the top has caramelized. Remove the pudding from the oven and serve it immediately.

Muhallabia

(Middle Eastern Almond Pudding)

This luscious, exotically flavored pudding is served in a glass dish and decorated with crystallized flowers.

6 portions

4	ounces blanched almonds		5	cups milk
3	tablespoons ground rice, purchased or home ground (see Introduction)		6	tablespoons superfine sugar
2	tablespoons cornstarch		3	tablespoons orange-flower water or rose water crystallized rose petals and violets

Grind the almonds and set aside. Mix the rice and cornstarch. Add a little of the milk and mix to a smooth paste. Combine the sugar and remaining milk and bring to a boil over moderate heat. Stir a little of the hot sugared milk into the starch mixture, then stir all of the starch mixture into the rest of the hot milk. Stir over very low heat until the mixture is thick enough to coat the back of the spoon. Add the orange-flower water or rose water. Cook for 2 minutes longer. Remove pudding from the heat and stir in the ground almonds. Turn into a glass dish and chill. Just before serving, decorate with rose petals and violets.

Normandy Apple Custard

4 to 6 portions

3	pounds cooking apples	¼	cup Calvados or applejack
½	teaspoon ground allspice	4	tablespoons butter
¼	teaspoon ground cloves	3	eggs
¾	cup granulated sugar	1	egg white
¼	cup cold water		

Wash, peel, seed and core the apples, and cut them into thin crescents. Place the apples and spices in a large heavy saucepan and toss to combine. Cover the pan, set it over low heat, and cook for 20 to 25 minutes, until the apples are very soft. Remove pan from the heat. Mash the apples with a fork, or purée in a food processor or blender. Return the purée to the pan and set again over low heat, uncovered, for 10 to 15 minutes, or until the purée is dry and stiff. Remove from the heat.

Place ½ cup of the sugar and the cold water in a heavy saucepan and set over low heat, stirring constantly, until the sugar is completely dissolved. Increase heat to high, bring the syrup to a boil, and cook 3 to 4 minutes, or until the syrup turns a rich brown. Watch closely and be careful not to overcook or the syrup will darken too much and become bitter. Warm a 4-cup mold and pour in the caramel, tilting and turning the mold to coat the insides evenly.

Preheat oven to 375°F. Beat the remaining ¼ cup sugar, the Calvados, butter and whole eggs into the apple purée. Beat the egg white until it holds soft peaks and fold it into the mixture. Spoon the custard into the caramel-lined mold and cover with aluminum foil. Set the mold in a baking pan and pour in enough boiling water to reach halfway up the sides of the mold. Bake the custard for 1¼ to 1½ hours, or until it is set and a knife inserted near the center comes out clean.

Remove the mold from the pan and cool it for 15 minutes. If you are serving it warm, turn it out at once onto a serving dish. If you are serving it cold, chill the mold in the refrigerator until just before serving. Unmold the custard and serve immediately.

Crème au Caramel

(Caramel Custard)

This custard is easier to turn out if made 24 hours in advance. Although it can be made in one large mold, it is easier to turn out of individual cocottes or dariole molds.

4 portions

½	cup plus 2 tablespoons superfine sugar	1	1-inch piece of vanilla bean, or 1 teaspoon vanilla extract
2	tablespoons cold water	2	large eggs
1½	cups milk	2	egg yolks

Preheat oven to 325°F. Place the ½ cup sugar and the cold water in a small heavy pan. Set the pan over low heat and stir constantly until the sugar melts. Increase heat to medium and cook the sugar without stirring until it turns a rich caramel color, about 2 minutes. Watch very carefully; the moment the sugar turns darker, remove pan from the heat. Hold a warmed 4-cup mold with a thick potholder. Quickly pour the hot caramel into the mold, turning it to coat the bottom and sides well. If you are using individual molds, coat each in turn with caramel.

Pour the milk into a heavy saucepan and add the vanilla bean. Scald over low heat until there are bubbles around the edge. Remove from the heat, cover, and set aside. Separate the 2 whole eggs. Place the yolks in a heatproof bowl and reserve the whites. Drop in remaining yolks and add the remaining 2 tablespoons sugar. Beat eggs and sugar together to mix thoroughly. Remove vanilla bean from the milk. (Wipe it dry and store for another use.) Pour the hot milk in a thin stream onto the egg mixture, stirring constantly without beating. If you have not used a vanilla bean, add the vanilla extract. Pour the custard through a fine sieve into the prepared mold or molds and cover with aluminum foil. Stand the mold or molds in a baking pan and pour in enough boiling water to come halfway up the sides of the mold. Bake the custard for 35 to 40 minutes, or until set in the center. Test the custard near the center with the point of a sharp knife; if it is ready, the knife will make a distinct mark, but if it is not, the custard will flow together again. Lift the mold from the baking pan and remove the foil. Cool custard thoroughly. When cold, cover again with foil and chill in the refrigerator for several hours.

To turn out the *crème au caramel*, invert a plate on top of the mold. Holding the plate and mold firmly together, turn them over. Lift off the mold. The liquid caramel sauce will run down the sides of custard.

Variations: The basic custard can be flavored with 3 ounces semisweet chocolate or 3 tablespoons instant coffee powder.

For a Viennese caramel, pour the caramel directly into the hot milk used to make the custard and bake in a ring mold. After turning out, fill the center with fresh fruits—strawberries, raspberries or peaches—or decorate with swirls of whipped cream.

Yugoslavian Rice Pudding

4 portions

2	teaspoons butter	2	large eggs
½	cup raw round-grain rice, such as Arborio	6	tablespoons peach jam
		1	can (15 ounces) peach slices
¼	cup superfine sugar	¾	cup sour cream
2½	cups milk	⅓	cup soft brown sugar
1¼	cups light cream	2	tablespoons slivered blanched almonds
½	teaspoon vanilla extract		

Preheat oven to 300°F. Coat a 6-cup flameproof baking dish with the butter. Place the rice, superfine sugar, milk, cream and vanilla in the buttered dish and stir well to mix. Place the rice mixture in the oven and bake for 3 hours. Remove dish from the oven and beat in the eggs. Set aside to cool.

Preheat broiler. Spread the peach jam over the cooled rice. Drain the peach slices and combine them with the sour cream. Spoon the peach mixture over the jam and then scatter the brown sugar and almonds on top. Place the dish under the broiler and broil 2 to 3 minutes, or until the top is lightly caramelized. Remove the dish from the broiler and serve at once.

Pots de Crème au Café

(Small Coffee Custards)

6 portions

2½	cups light cream	2	tablespoons Coffee Essence (see Volume 1 Index)
1	egg		
5	egg yolks		
3	tablespoons sugar	2	tablespoons brandy

Preheat oven to 325°F. Heat the cream in a saucepan over low heat until bubbles appear around the edges. Remove pan from the heat and set aside. In a mixing bowl beat the whole egg, yolks, sugar, coffee essence and brandy together with a wooden spoon until they are just combined. Stirring constantly with the wooden spoon, gradually pour the hot cream onto the egg mixture, beating until everything is well blended. Pour the mixture through a sieve into another bowl. Then divide it among 6 small *pots de crème*, custard cups, or individual ramekins. Place the filled containers in a baking pan and pour in enough boiling water to come halfway up the sides of the containers. Cover each dish or cup with aluminum foil or the pots with their own covers. Bake the custards for 25 to 30 minutes, or until lightly set and a knife inserted near the center comes out clean. Cool the baked custards, then chill in the refrigerator before serving.

Pots de Crème au Chocolat

(Small Chocolate Custards)

6 portions

8	ounces semisweet cooking chocolate	1	large egg
1¼	cups light cream	4	egg yolks
1¼	cups milk	4	tablespoons superfine sugar
			whipped cream (optional)

Preheat oven to 325°F. In a saucepan set over very low heat, melt the chocolate with the cream and milk. Stir occasionally with a wooden spoon. Remove pan from the heat and set it aside for 10 minutes to let the chocolate cool. Beat the whole egg and the yolks until very well blended, then beat in the sugar until the mixture is thick and lemon-colored. Pour ½ cup of the milk and chocolate mixture into the egg mixture, stirring all the while, then turn the warmed egg mixture into the rest of the chocolate mixture and stir to blend well, without adding too much froth. Strain the mixture through a fine sieve into 6 *pots de crème* or custard cups. Cover them with their tops or with foil and set the pots in a pan of boiling water that comes halfway up the sides of the pots. Bake the custards for 15 to 25 minutes, until a knife blade inserted near the center comes out clean. Remove pots from the water, uncover, and let them cool. Chill until ready to serve. Garnish with whipped cream, or serve plain.

Pumpkin and Caramel Flan

8 to 10 portions

2	cups puréed pumpkin, fresh or canned		1¼	cups milk
2	teaspoons ground ginger		1	lemon
3	tablespoons flour		1⅓	cups superfine sugar
5	large eggs		¼	cup cold water

Preheat oven to 325°F. Combine the pumpkin, ginger, flour and eggs in a large mixing bowl. Beat with a wooden spoon until the ingredients are thoroughly blended. Set the milk over moderate heat until bubbles appear around the edges. Juice the lemon. Remove milk from the heat and stir in ¾ cup of the sugar and the lemon juice. Continue stirring until the sugar is dissolved. Strain the milk mixture into the pumpkin mixture, stirring constantly.

Pour the cold water into a heavy saucepan. Add the remaining sugar and dissolve over moderate heat, stirring constantly. Increase heat to moderately high and boil the syrup until it is a rich caramel brown. Do not allow the caramel to become too dark or it will burn and taste bitter. Pour the caramel immediately into a warmed 6-cup mold.

Tip and rotate the mold to coat the bottom and sides evenly before it cools and hardens.

Pour the pumpkin mixture into the mold. Set the mold in a baking pan with enough boiling water to reach halfway up the sides of the mold. Bake the custard for 1½ hours, or until it is set and a knife inserted in the center comes out clean. Remove the mold from the water and let the custard cool, then cover the mold with foil and chill in the refrigerator for at least 3 hours, or overnight.

To unmold the flan, invert a serving dish on the mold. Holding dish and mold firmly together, turn them over and give the mold a good shake. The flan should slide out easily. The caramel will run down the sides of the custard to make a sauce.

Peaches and Cream Pudding

6 to 8 portions

4	large fresh peaches	½	cup slivered blanched almonds
1¼	cups light cream	½	cup superfine sugar
1¼	cups heavy cream	6	egg yolks
4	pieces of crystallized ginger, about 1 ounce altogether	⅔	cup dark brown sugar

Blanch the peaches in boiling water for about 30 seconds. Peel, slice them, and discard pits. Combine both creams in a saucepan and heat until bubbles form around the edges; set aside. Mince the ginger. Arrange the sliced peaches and the almonds in a deep 6-cup flameproof serving dish. Beat the superfine sugar and egg yolks with a whisk or rotary or electric beater until light and smooth. Gradually beat in the scalded creams. Pour the mixture into a large heavy saucepan. Set pan over low heat and stir constantly with a wooden spoon until the custard is thick enough to coat the spoon. Do not let the custard boil. Remove pan from heat and beat the custard at slow speed for 2 more minutes. Strain custard through a fine sieve and stir in the crystallized ginger. Pour the custard over the peaches and almonds. Let the custard cool at room temperature, then chill in the refrigerator for 2 hours.

Preheat broiler. Remove serving dish from refrigerator and sprinkle the surface of the custard with the brown sugar. Place the dish under the broiler and broil until the sugar caramelizes, taking care not to let it burn. Serve immediately.

Chocolate Cream

6 portions

2½	cups milk	1½	envelopes (4½ scant teaspoons) unflavored gelatin
4	large eggs	⅛	teaspoon salt
1	tablespoon butter	2	tablespoons brandy
5	tablespoons superfine sugar	4	ounces semisweet cooking chocolate
3	tablespoons flour	1	cup heavy cream
1	teaspoon vanilla extract	6	shelled walnut halves
6	tablespoons cold water		

Pour the milk into a saucepan and set over moderate heat until bubbles form at the edges of the pan. Remove pan from the heat. Separate the eggs. Cream the butter. In a mixing bowl beat the egg yolks and 4 tablespoons of the sugar with a whisk or rotary or electric beater until thick and pale yellow. Beat in the flour, then the scalded milk, a few drops at a time. When all the milk has been beaten in, pour the mixture into a saucepan and cook over moderate heat, stirring constantly, for 2 minutes. Remove pan from the heat and beat in the vanilla and the butter. Strain the custard through a fine sieve into a large bowl.

Place the cold water in a saucepan, sprinkle the gelatin over it, and leave for 5 minutes. Dissolve the gelatin over low heat until the solution is clear. Scrape the gelatin into the warm custard and combine thoroughly.

Beat the egg whites and salt until they form soft peaks. Sprinkle in the remaining tablespoon of sugar and beat until the whites become stiff and glossy. Place the brandy in a cup. Break the chocolate into small pieces and drop into the brandy. Set the cup in a pan of hot water and place over low heat until the chocolate is melted. Stir to combine with the brandy. Using a metal spoon or rubber spatula, fold the melted chocolate into the custard, then fold in the beaten egg whites. Spoon the chocolate cream into a serving bowl or individual glass bowls, cover with foil, and refrigerate for 3 hours.

Just before serving whip the heavy cream until stiff. Decorate the pudding with the whipped cream and the walnut halves.

Riz à l'Impératrice

(Empress Rice)

This rich dessert was first concocted for the Empress Eugénie of France.

6 portions

1	tablespoon butter	2	tablespoons kirsch
½	cup raw round-grain rice, such as Arborio	½	cup cold water
¼	cup sugar	2	envelopes (2 scant tablespoons) unflavored gelatin
3¾	cups milk	3	egg yolks
1½	teaspoons vanilla extract	1	cup Custard Sauce (see Index)*
2	tablespoons chopped candied peel	1¼	cups heavy cream
2	tablespoons chopped glacé cherries	2	tablespooms apricot jam

Preheat oven to 300°F. Coat a 6-cup baking dish with the butter. Place the rice, sugar, milk and vanilla in the dish and stir to combine. Bake the pudding in the oven for 3 hours.

Meanwhile, place the candied peel and glacé cherries in a small bowl, pour the kirsch over them, and leave to macerate at room temperature. Pour the cold water into a small saucepan, sprinkle the gelatin over it, and soak for 5 minutes. Set the saucepan over low heat until the gelatin dissolves. Remove from the heat.

Remove the baking dish from the oven, cool for 10 minutes and beat in the egg yolks, one by one. Add the dissolved gelatin and mix well. Set aside to cool at room temperature for another 10 minutes. Beat in the macerated fruits along with any kirsch that hasn't been absorbed by

them. With a metal spoon or rubber spatula fold in the custard sauce. Whip the cream until stiff and fold it into the pudding.

Coat the inside of a 2-quart mold lightly with the apricot jam. Spoon the rice mixture into the mold, smoothing it down with the back of a wooden spoon. Cover lightly. Chill the mold in the refrigerator for 2 hours, or until the mixture has set.

Remove the mold from the refrigerator and dip the bottom quickly into hot water. Invert a serving dish over the mold. Holding dish and mold firmly together, turn them over. Serve immediately.

*When making the sauce omit the crystallized ginger.

Gus-Khrustalny

(Russian Cream Pudding with Almonds)

6 to 8 portions

1	teaspoon butter	¼	cup uncooked semolina
1¼	cups heavy cream	5	tablespoons sugar
⅔	cup blanched almonds	½	teaspoon vanilla extract
2	cups light cream	½	cup apricot jam

Preheat broiler. Use the butter to coat a deep pie dish. Pour the heavy cream into a shallow flameproof dish and place it under the broiler. Heat the cream until a burned skin forms. Remove the dish from the broiler and transfer the skin to a plate. Return dish to the broiler and continue cooking the cream and removing the skin as it forms, until almost all the cream has been used. Set the cream skins aside.

Place the almonds on the broiler pan and toast them until browned. Turn them over and brown the other side. Watch carefully to prevent burning. Remove the toasted almonds from the broiler and chop them. Adjust oven heat to 375°F. Pour the light cream into a saucepan and add the semolina. Heat together over low heat, stirring constantly, until the mixture comes to a boil and thickens. Remove pan from the heat and stir in 4 tablespoons of the sugar, the vanilla and the chopped almonds.

Place a layer of the burned cream skin in the buttered pie dish. Cover it with a layer of the semolina mixture, then with a layer of jam. Repeat layering until all ingredients are used. Sprinkle the remaining tablespoon of sugar over the surface of the pudding and slide the dish into the oven. Bake the pudding for 20 minutes, or until it is set and golden brown. Serve immediately.

Crème Brûlée

(Custard with Burned Sugar Topping)

A very old dessert that appears in an English cookbook of 200 years ago and is probably even older than that, crème brûlée has recently been enjoying renewed popularity. Ideally, preparations for this dessert should be begun the night before it is served.

6 to 8 portions

1	cup light cream	4	large eggs
1	cup heavy cream	3	tablespoons superfine sugar
1	2-inch piece of vanilla bean, or 1 teaspoon vanilla extract	⅔	cup brown sugar

Pour both light and heavy cream into a saucepan and add the vanilla bean, if using. Set the saucepan over low heat until there are bubbles around the edges. Remove the scalded cream from the heat, cover, and leave to infuse. Separate the eggs and reserve the whites. Beat the egg yolks and superfine sugar together until thick. Remove the vanilla bean from the cream. (Wipe dry and store for another use.) Add vanilla extract if vanilla bean has not been used. Half-fill the lower pan of a double boiler with hot water and set over low heat. Make sure the water does not boil. Pour the hot cream in a thin stream onto the egg-yolk mixture, stirring all the time with a wooden spoon. Strain the mixture through a sieve into the top pan of the double boiler. Set the top pan in the bottom, making sure that the bottom of the top pan does not touch the water. Cook the custard slowly, stirring constantly with a wooden spoon, for about 15 minutes. The custard is ready when it reaches the consistency of very thick cream and leaves a coating on the spoon. Strain it into a straight-sided flameproof baking dish or into individual soufflé dishes. Let cool to room temperature and chill in the refrigerator for 4 hours or, preferably, overnight.

About 2½ hours before you plan to serve the custard, preheat the broiler. Remove the custard from the refrigerator. Sieve the brown sugar over it in an even layer. Make sure the surface is completely covered. Slide the dish under the broiler, placing it as close as possible to the heat source. Let the sugar melt and become a pale gold brown, about 2 minutes, and immediately remove from the heat. Do not let it overcook, or the sugar will become bitter and black. Let the custard cool at room temperature, then chill in the refrigerator for no more than 2 to 3 hours before serving. If it is stored longer, the sugar will melt into the custard and there will be no contrast between the crisp sugar topping and the soft custard.

Hasty Pudding

In England hasty pudding was most commonly made with flour or oatmeal and brown sugar, but early colonists in America had neither, so when they made a *sweet version of this they made it with corn meal and molasses, or sometimes maple syrup.*

4 portions

4	tablespoons plus 1 teaspoon butter
3	cups milk
⅓	cup yellow corn meal
⅓	cup molasses

½	teaspoon grated nutmeg
½	teaspoon ground cinnamon
½	teaspoon salt
	Heavy cream (optional)
	Maple syrup (optional)

Preheat oven to 350°F. Use the teaspoon of butter to coat a 4-cup baking dish. Pour 1 cup milk into a large bowl and sprinkle in the corn meal. Stir until corn meal is completely moistened. Melt the remaining 4 tablespoons butter in a saucepan, then pour in remaining 2 cups milk and heat just to a simmer. Pour milk and butter onto the moistened corn meal and stir until all the milk seems to be absorbed. Return the entire mixture to the saucepan and simmer over low heat until the batter comes away from the sides of the pan. Mix in the molasses, spices and salt. Turn the pudding into the buttered baking dish and smooth the top. Cover the dish with foil. Set it in a pan and pour simmering water around it and slide it into the oven. Cook for 1 hour, or longer if you like a firmer pudding. Serve hot, with plain cream or maple syrup.

Duchess Pudding

4 portions

8	tablespoons plus 2 teaspoons butter	2	eggs
½	cup sugar	⅓	cup raisins
1½	cups all-purpose flour	⅓	cup chopped blanched almonds
1½	teaspoons baking powder	¼	teaspoon almond extract
		1	to 3 tablespoons milk

Use 1 teaspoon of the butter to coat a 4-cup pudding dish. Use the other teaspoon to coat a sheet of foil. Cream the 8 tablespoons butter and the sugar together until pale and fluffy. Sift the flour and baking powder together. Add 1 egg and 1 tablespoon of the sifted flour to the butter and sugar mixture and beat briskly to combine. Add another egg and another tablespoon of the sifted mixture and again beat briskly. Fold in the remaining flour mixture, the raisins and almonds. Add the almond extract and enough milk to give the batter the consistency of a drop-cookie batter. Spoon the batter into the prepared dish, rounding the top slightly. Pleat the foil and tie it, buttered side toward the pudding, over the dish.

Half-fill a steamer or large saucepan with water and bring to a boil over high heat. Place the pudding dish on a steamer rack or on a trivet in the saucepan. Reduce heat to moderate to keep the water just boiling, and steam the pudding for 1½ hours. Replenish the boiling water as needed.

Remove the dish from the steamer. Uncover the pudding and invert it onto a warmed serving dish. Serve at once.

Tyrolean Semolina

6 portions

2½	cups milk	1	lemon
4	tablespoons sugar	1	apple
¾	cup uncooked semolina	3	ounces small seedless grapes
1	envelope (1 scant tablespoon) unflavored gelatin	1	tablespoon brandy
		½	cup heavy cream
1	orange	1	large egg white
		1	tablespoon flavorless oil

Pour the milk into the top pan of a double boiler. Add the sugar and sprinkle the semolina on the milk. Set the top pan over hot water and cook the mixture, stirring from time to time, until it is thickened and smooth. Remove from the heat and cool.

Lightly oil a plain 4-cup mold. Squeeze the orange and lemon. Place the orange juice in a small pan, sprinkle gelatin over it and leave for 5 minutes. Peel, core and dice the apple and toss the pieces in the lemon juice to prevent discolora-tion. Wash and peel the grapes. Dissolve the gelatin over low heat. Cool it, then stir it thoroughly into the semolina mixture. Add the diced apple, the peeled grapes and the brandy and stir well to combine. Whip the cream until it just holds its shape and fold into the mixture. Beat the egg white until it stands in soft peaks and fold it into the mixture. Turn the pudding into the mold and chill for 2 hours before turning it out.

Viennese Fruit Custard

6 portions

2½	cups milk	2	egg yolks
1	cup sugar	2	tablespoons chopped mixed candied fruits
1	1-inch piece of vanilla bean or 1 teaspoon vanilla extract	1	orange
		⅓	cup Sugar Syrup (see Volume 6 Index)
¼	cup cold water		
2	eggs		

Pour the milk into a heavy saucepan and add ½ cup of the sugar. Bring to a boil over moderate heat, stirring occasionally. When the sugar is dissolved, add the vanilla bean. Cover the pan, remove from heat, and leave to infuse for 20 minutes.

Place the remaining ½ cup sugar and the cold water in a heavy saucepan and set over low heat, stirring constantly, until the sugar is completely dissolved. Increase heat to high and bring the syrup to a boil. Cook for 3 to 4 minutes, until the syrup turns a nut-brown color. Watch closely and be careful not to overcook or it will darken too much and become bitter. Pour the caramelized syrup into a warmed 4-cup decorative ovenproof mold and turn and tip the mold to coat all sides evenly with the caramel.

Preheat oven to 325°F. Beat the whole eggs and the yolks with a whisk or rotary or electric beater until they become thick and pale yellow. Strain the milk. (Dry the vanilla bean and reserve for another use.) Pour the milk onto the eggs, beating constantly. If you have not used the vanilla bean, add the vanilla extract. Put the mixture through a fine wire sieve into a mixing bowl and stir in the chopped candied fruits. Pour the mixture into the prepared mold. Place the mold in a deep-sided baking pan and pour in enough boiling water to come halfway up the sides of the mold. Bake the custard for 40 minutes, or until set and a knife inserted near the center comes out clean. Remove the mold from the pan and set aside to cool completely. When the custard is cool, chill it in the refrigerator for 1 hour.

While the custard is chilling, make the garnish. Peel the orange, removing any white pith. Slice the orange, and remove any pits. Poach the slices in the sugar syrup until the slices are shiny and glazed. Set the slices aside to cool.

When ready to serve, unmold the custard and decorate the top with the glazed orange slices. Serve immediately.

Part Five

NEW YEAR'S DAY OPEN HOUSE

"My best of wishes for . . . your happy New Year, your long lives and your true prosperities. Worth twenty pound good if they are delivered as I send them. . . . Here's a final prescription added, To be taken for life."

—Charles Dickens

In terms of friendships and family and all the ties that bind, a New Year's Day open house can be the sweetest and most pleasurable party on the calendar. Whether you are celebrating in a skyscraper or in Norman Rockwell country—snow, roasted chestnuts, a crackling fire and a fat marmalade tabby before it—this is a day to warm hearts and be close to those you love. If New Year's Eve is the time for elegance or frenzy, New Year's Day is the time for simplicity and hominess. Beguile your guests with coziness and comfort instead of razzle-dazzle.

Although this is a bountiful meal, the major part of the work can be done ahead of time so you can play host or hostess instead of cook. Just as the gleaming mountains of honey-gilded ham and crusty brown chicken pieces require little last-minute attention, so too have all the other dishes been designed to keep you out of the kitchen and enjoying the occasion as much as your guests. To guarantee this, start your preparations well in advance. If you like, follow the schedule we suggest by making the potted cheese, the soup and the cranberry filling three days ahead of time (all will profit from the period of waiting; flavors will marry and mellow). Two days ahead make the crackers and store them airtight, make the pâte sucrée and refrigerate it, and bake the ginger-bread. One day ahead, make the cranberry and dried fruit tartlets (cover well and leave at cool room temperature), make and chill the custard sauce and then complete the trifle and refrigerate it. Early on the day of the party, coat the chicken pieces, make and chill the coleslaw—do not dress it—and remove the Stilton from the refrigerator. Several hours before the party, bake the ham, then the corn pudding and the chicken after that; and shortly before your guests arrive, prepare the biscuit batter, make the mulled cider, and set the soup to heat. Yes, there's a lot to do, even for this down-home meal, but spread out over three days you should be able to handle the work with aplomb.

Because this will be a day when you want your guests to feel that your home is their home, your house should look inviting but informal. Leave your best linens in the closet and use a simple cloth—perhaps a checkered one—or convert an interesting piece of fabric or a wall hanging into a tablecloth for the day. Keep the flowers simple as well—daisies or bittersweet would be beautiful, or perhaps just a lush bunch of evergreen branches or holly. The food will be all the additional ornamentation you need—this is an exceptionally attractive buffet.

Welcome your guests in from the cold by offering them mulled cider—with or without the applejack—and then give them the run of the kitchen so they can freely help themselves to more. (The kitchen is an extension of this party, for it is there—

unless you have two large and attractive electric crockpots to place on the table—that the cider and soup will spend the afternoon, kept warm on a low flame, ladles and gleaming glass mugs resting nearby.) Do your last chores—pop the buttermilk biscuits in the oven, dress the coleslaw and whip the cream—and then join your guests to have the pleasure of their company and to give them the pleasure of yours. Relax and settle back to a convivial time of warmth and plenty, content in the knowledge that you have provided your guests with a sweet afternoon's respite between the demands of the old year and the as yet unknown claims of the new.

NEW YEAR'S DAY OPEN HOUSE FOR TWENTY-FIVE

Hot Mulled Cider with Applejack
Bean, Spinach and Tomato Soup
Honey-Glazed Baked Ham with Buttermilk Biscuits
Oven-Fried Cayenne Chicken
Red and Green Cabbage Slaw with Lemon Dressing
Corn Pudding
Cranberry-Orange Tartlets
Tartlets of Dried Fruits
Gingerbread-Apple Trifle with Custard Sauce
Assorted Winter Grapes with Stilton Cheese and Pumpernickel Bread
English Potted Cheese with Water Crackers (see Index)

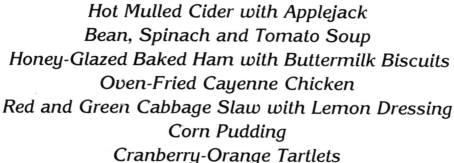

MARKET LIST

Meat and Poultry

1 fully cooked bone-in ham, 11 to 15 pounds	5 broiler-fryer chickens, each about 3½ pounds

Fruit and Vegetables

7 to 9 medium-size onions	1 green cabbage (½ head—1¼ pounds)	2 bags (12 ounces each) fresh cranberries
1 pound carrots	2 heads garlic	2 apples (6 to 8 ounces each) plus 4½ pounds firm apples such as Granny Smith, Rome Beauty or Golden Delicious
8 ounces spinach leaves	Flat-leaf Italian parsley	
1 large bunch of broccoli (2½ pounds)	1 orange plus 1 seedless (navel) orange	
1 red cabbage (½ head—1¼ pounds)	4 lemons	

Dairy

Double Gloucester,
   Cheshire or sharp
   Cheddar cheese (3 pounds)
Stilton cheese (1 wheel)

Parmesan cheese (½ to ¾
   pound)
Unsalted butter (6 pounds)
Buttermilk (1 quart)

Half-and-half (3 pints)
Heavy cream (½ pint) plus
   cream for whipping (optional)
Eggs (1 dozen plus 8)

Staples

All-purpose flour (13½
   cups) plus unbleached
   white (1⅓ cups)
Dark brown sugar (1¾ cups)
Granulated sugar (3 cups)
Superfine sugar (4 tablespoons)
Baking powder
Baking soda
Dried Great Northern or
   navy beans (2 pounds)
Canned whole tomatoes
   (32 ounces)
Canned cream-style corn
   (4 cans, 17 ounces each)

Olive oil
Vegetable oil
Light vegetable oil
Honey (1 cup)
Molasses (2 cups)
Golden raisins (6 ounces)
Dark raisins (6 ounces)
Pitted dried prunes (6
   ounces)
Pitted dried apricots (6
   ounces)
Orange or apple juice
Bacon fat
Dijon-style mustard

Salt
Freshly ground pepper
Cayenne pepper
Ground ginger
Ground mace
Ground cloves
Whole cloves
Whole allspice
Cinnamon sticks (12)
Freshly grated nutmeg
Dry mustard
Vanilla extract
Brandy (2 tablespoons)
Sweet sherry (1½ cups)

Specialty Items

Lard (1 cup)
Hot mustard
Sweet mustard

Pumpernickel bread
Pecans (about 4 ounces
   shelled)

Crystallized ginger (about ½ cup)
Sweet cider (8 quarts)
Applejack (1 bottle)

American Sparkling Wines

Although Champagne is the best known and the greatest of the sparkling wines, there are, of course, many others worth investigating. In recent years, American wines in this category have begun to increase in popularity and they are a perfect accompaniment to this largely American meal, a festive carryover from the revelry of New Year's Eve but far more in keeping with the leisurely, informal atmosphere of this New Year's Day open house.

Start your party off with a bang by serving your guests a magnum of Domaine Chandon Napa Valley Brut, a very dry California beauty, or the slightly fruitier Blanc de Noirs. There is something magical about an oversized bottle of bubbly (a magnum contains two regular-size bottles), its appearance sending even apathetic types into a happy frenzy of excitement and anticipation. (There are also larger-size bottles—the Jeroboam, which holds 4 bottles, the Rehoboam, 6 bottles, the Methuselah, 8 bottles, the Salmanazar, 12 bottles, the Balthazar, 16 bottles, and the Nebuchadnezzar, 20 bottles—but they are very hard to find. Their curious names were developed around 1850 or 1860, it is thought, by British wine brokers, who felt that these grand bottles deserved equally grand names and so turned to the Bible for most of them.)

Drink the Domaine Chandon throughout the meal or, if you prefer, use it as an aperitif and then bring out a lovely Hans Kornell Champagne Rosé (not really a Champagne, which can't be made outside the French region of that name, but a sparkling wine produced by the same bottle-fermented method as a true Champagne.) And don't be misled by the color into thinking this champagne rosé is just a giggle; it's a serious and beautiful wine.

Dessert demands a slightly sweeter wine, perhaps a Hans Kornell Sparkling Muscat Alexandria, redolent with the distinctive floral aroma and flavor of the muscat grape.

Hot Mulled Cider with Applejack

about 30 portions

8	quarts sweet cider	1	tablespoon whole allspice
6	tablespoons dark brown sugar	12	sticks cinnamon
			freshly grated nutmeg
1	tablespoon whole cloves	1	bottle applejack

Combine cider and sugar in a large kettle, preferably stainless or enamel-lined. Rinse a square of cheesecloth, place the cloves and allspice in it, tie and add to the cider along with the cinnamon sticks. Bring to a boil over medium heat, adjust heat to maintain mixture at a simmer and leave for 15 to 20 minutes.

Turn heat down as low as possible to keep the mulled cider warm. To serve, ladle the cider into mugs and offer your guests the applejack so they can spike the cider to their taste.

Bean, Spinach and Tomato Soup

This completely vegetarian bean soup can be made 1 to 3 days before serving. In fact, like many starchy dishes, it actually improves if made ahead.

about 25 portions

2	pounds dried Great Northern or navy beans	1	tablespoon salt
			freshly ground black pepper
6	to 8 medium-size onions	32	ounces canned whole tomatoes
10	garlic cloves	8	ounces spinach leaves
4	tablespoons vegetable oil		freshly grated Parmesan cheese
1	pound carrots		

Place the beans in a very large pot and add 2 quarts of water. Heat to boiling, stir once, and boil hard for 2 minutes. Skim foam from the top. Remove from heat and let stand, covered, for 1 hour.

Peel and chop the onions. Peel the garlic and cut into slivers. Combine the onion, garlic and oil in a large heavy saucepan. Cover and cook over very low heat, stirring occasionally, until onions are very soft and just until they are a pale beige and slightly caramelized, about 25 minutes. Do not let onions brown.

Add onion mixture to the beans and soaking liquid. Add 6 quarts water, heat to boiling over high heat, and stir well. Reduce heat to low and simmer, uncovered, for 2 hours, stirring occasionally.

Scrape the carrots and cut into ¼-inch slices. Add carrots, salt and pepper to taste. Simmer for 30 minutes.

Drain the tomatoes in a sieve set over a bowl to catch the juices. Seed the tomatoes and rinse individually under cold running water to remove any remaining seeds. Add the tomatoes to the reserved tomato juice. Press any pulp left in the sieve with the back of a spoon to extract the juice; add to tomatoes. Wash the spinach leaves thoroughly. Stem spinach and chop leaves. Stir the spinach and the tomatoes and their juice into the soup. Cook the soup, uncovered, over low heat for 30 minutes. Season to taste with additional salt and pepper.

To serve, ladle soup into mugs or bowls and sprinkle with cheese.

Honey-Glazed Baked Ham

Although this ham does not have to be cooked before eating, the meat will be more flavorful if it is. The ham can be prepared hours ahead of time and served at room temperature.

22 to 30 portions

1	fully cooked bone-in ham, 11 to 15 pounds
1	orange
1	cup honey
1	tablespoon Dijon-style mustard

Preheat oven to 325°F. Place the ham on a rack, round side up, in a large roasting pan. If there is a skin covering the fatty surface of the ham, remove it by slipping a knife underneath and peeling it off. If necessary, trim the fat so there is no more than ½ inch.

Bake the ham for 10 to 12 minutes a pound. One hour before the ham is ready, grate the orange rind to measure 1 tablespoon. Combine the rind, honey and mustard in a small saucepan and heat, stirring often, until warm. Brush this glaze generously over the surface of the ham, and repeat frequently as ham bakes. Thirty minutes before the ham is ready, remove it from the oven and score the fat in a criss-cross pattern to a depth of about ⅛ inch. Brush with glaze and return to the oven. Cook, basting frequently, until the ham is golden and crusty and has reached an internal temperature of 130°F. Serve at room temperature.

Buttermilk Biscuits

Make twice this many biscuits for your party, but do not double the recipe or the biscuits will not turn out as well. Simply make two separate batches and then bake them all at once (and don't forget to serve them with lots of unsalted butter).

18 to 20 biscuits

	bacon fat
3	cups all-purpose flour
1	tablespoon baking powder
1	teaspoon salt
½	teaspoon baking soda
½	cup lard, chilled
1	to 1¼ cups buttermilk
2	tablespoons unsalted butter

Preheat oven to 450°F. Coat a baking pan, 10½ × 15½ inches, with bacon fat.

Sift the flour, baking powder, salt and baking soda into a large bowl. Cut in the lard until mixture resembles coarse meal. Gradually add buttermilk, tossing the mixture with a fork as you pour. Toss only until the dry ingredients are evenly moistened. Flour your hands and scrape mixture out of bowl onto a lightly floured work surface. Give the dough three or four turns, kneading it into a solid mass. Be careful not to overwork the dough. Lightly flour your work surface.

With a floured rolling pin, roll dough out to a thickness of approximately ½ inch. Cut dough into rounds with a 2-inch biscuit cutter. Press scraps together to form additional biscuits. Melt the butter. Place biscuits on prepared baking pan. Brush the surface of biscuits lightly with melted butter.

Bake the biscuits on the center rack of oven for 15 to 20 minutes, or until lightly browned. Before serving, cool on a rack for 5 minutes.

If biscuits are baked ahead, wrap loosely in foil and reheat in a 350°F oven for 10 minutes. Cool briefly and serve.

Oven-Fried Cayenne Chicken

The chicken pieces can all be coated and arranged on the pans hours before oven-frying and serving time. Cover them lightly. If refrigeration space is limited, leave them out in a cool space until ready to place in oven. Plan to cook them just enough ahead of time to leave the oven free for baking the biscuits. This chicken is delicious straight from the oven but it's equally delicious warm or at room temperature, so don't worry about the wait. Just set it aside—uncovered—in a warm place.

makes 50 pieces

5	broiler-fryers, each about		5	cups all-purpose flour
	3½ pounds		3½	teaspoons salt
1¼	pounds butter		2½	teaspoons cayenne pepper

Cut each chicken into 10 pieces—2 legs, 2 thighs, 2 wings, and the breast cut in half lengthwise and then crosswise to form 4 pieces. Preheat oven to 400°F. Melt the butter. Generously brush two very large roasting pans with a layer of melted butter.

Combine the flour, salt and cayenne pepper in a plastic bag and shake well to mix. Shake chicken pieces, one at a time, in the flour mixture to coat; shake off excess flour. Generously brush chicken pieces with melted butter or dip them in it, covering them on all sides. One at a time, return the coated chicken pieces to the bag with the flour mixture, and coat generously with flour. Arrange chicken in baking pans, leaving room around each piece.

Bake for 45 to 60 minutes, carefully turning pieces several times with a metal spatula, until very well browned on all sides. (You must use a spatula to turn the pieces or the crispy, delicious crust will stick to the bottom of the pan instead of to the chicken.)

Red and Green Cabbage Slaw with Lemon Dressing

makes about 20 cups

2½	pounds broccoli (1 large bunch)		¼	teaspoon freshly ground black pepper
3	lemons		½	head of red cabbage, about 1¼ pounds
1	small garlic clove		½	head of green cabbage, about 1¼ pounds
½	cup olive oil			
½	cup light vegetable oil		1	medium-size onion
2	tablespoons cold water		¼	cup chopped flat-leaf (Italian) parsley
½	teaspoon salt			

Trim the flowerets from the broccoli stalks. You should have about 3 cups of flowerets. Reserve the stalks for another use. Place broccoli in a vegetable steamer set over boiling water, cover, and steam until crisp-tender, about 3 minutes. Refresh under cold running water, drain, and let cool.

With a vegetable peeler, cut 3 strips of lemon rind (yellow part only) from one of the lemons. They should be about 3 inches long and ½ inch wide. Blanch the strips of lemon rind in a small amount of boiling water for 2 minutes; drain them and blot dry. Cut the strips crosswise into very thin slivers.

Squeeze the remaining lemons to measure ⅓ cup juice; remove seeds. Peel and chop the garlic. Whisk together the oils, lemon juice, water, salt, pepper and garlic in a small bowl until blended; stir in slivered lemon rind. Set dressing aside until ready to use.

Remove the outer leaves of the cabbage, cut each cabbage half in two, and core each piece. Cut the cabbage into thin slivers using a large sharp knife or the slicing blade of a food processor, or shred on the large-hole side of a grater. Peel and halve the onion and cut into thin slices. Combine the cabbage, onion and broccoli flowerets in a large bowl. Refrigerate until ready to proceed.

Just before serving, add the dressing and toss to coat evenly. Add parsley, toss to combine, and transfer to a large glass bowl.

Corn Pudding

This creamy corn pudding is delicious served warm, but is also wonderful at room temperature.

about 25 portions

8	eggs		½	teaspoon salt
2	cups half-and-half		4	cans cream-style corn, 17
½	teaspoon freshly ground black pepper			ounces each

Generously butter two 2-quart shallow baking dishes. Preheat oven to 350°F.

Place the eggs, half-and-half, pepper and salt in a large bowl and whisk until thoroughly blended. Add the corn and stir to blend. Divide the mixture between the prepared baking dishes. Set each baking dish in a larger pan and carefully pour boiling water into the larger dish to a depth of about 1 inch. Bake for 40 to 50 minutes, or until set. Remove puddings from the water bath and place on a wire rack to cool. Serve warm or at room temperature.

Cranberry-Orange Tartlets

*If you don't have enough tartlet tins, fill and bake as
many as you have and repeat until all tartlets are made.
Prepare the pâte sucrée the day before.*

**15 individual tartlets,
or two 8-inch tarts**

2 bags fresh cranberries, 12 ounces each	1 recipe Pâte Sucrée (see Volume 2 Index)
1 seedless navel orange	whipped cream (optional)
2 cups sugar	

Empty one bag of the cranberries into a colander, rinse and pick over, removing stems or bruised berries. Turn into a bowl and set aside. Repeat with the remaining bag of cranberries and turn into a second bowl.

Cut the orange into ½-inch chunks or slices. Place half of one bowl of cranberries in a food processor or meat grinder, add half of the orange slices, and process or grind until coarse. Transfer the mixture to a large deep skillet. Repeat with the cranberries remaining in the first bowl and remaining orange slices and add to the skillet. Add remaining bowl of whole cranberries and sugar and mix until thoroughly combined with ground mixture. Cover skillet and set over medium heat for about 5 minutes, or until the berries begin to exude juices and the sugar begins to dissolve. Uncover and cook over medium-high heat, stirring occasionally, until the whole berries begin to pop and the mixture thickens, about 10 minutes. Do not overcook. Remove from heat and set aside at room temperature until completely cool.

While the berries are cooling, roll out the pastry dough and fit into tartlet tins, 3½ inches × ¾ inch, or two 8-inch loose-bottomed tart rings. Preheat oven to 450°F. Arrange the tart pans on a large baking sheet. Fill each tartlet with approximately ¼ cup of filling, or divide the filling between the two 8-inch tarts. Bake for 10 minutes, then reduce oven temperature to 350°F. Bake for about 35 minutes, or until the pastry is golden brown. Place on wire racks until cool enough to handle, about 20 minutes.

Carefully loosen the tartlets or tarts from tins by using the tip of a sharp knife to separate the pastry from the sides of the tins. Then carefully invert the tart into the palm of one hand. Press in on the bottom of the pan with the thumb of the other hand to release the bottom of the pastry shell. Lift out of the pan and carefully place tartlet right side up on a wire rack to continue cooling. Repeat with remaining tartlets. If you have made 8-inch tarts, after loosening pastry from sides of tart tins, set tins on the tops of wide-mouth jars and slip tart rings down around them, leaving tarts and bottoms of rings on top of jars. Set tarts on a rack. To serve, arrange on a large attractive tray or platter. If desired, place a large bowl of whipped cream near the tartlets so guests can help themselves.

Tartlets of Dried Fruits

*If you don't have enough tartlet tins, fill and bake as
many as you have and repeat until all tartlets are made.
Prepare the pâte sucrée the day before.*

**15 individual tartlets,
or two 8-inch tarts**

1 cup dried apricots, about 6 ounces	2 medium-size apples (6 to 8 ounces each)
1 cup pitted dried prunes, about 6 ounces	½ cup orange or apple juice
1 cup golden raisins, about 6 ounces	⅓ cup packed dark brown sugar
½ cup dark raisins, about 3 ounces	2 tablespoons brandy
1 recipe Pâte Sucrée (see Volume 2 Index)	1 cup chopped pecans, about 4 ounces
	whipped cream (optional)

Halve apricots. Combine the prunes, golden raisins, apricots and dark raisins in a saucepan; add water just to cover. Cook over medium-high heat until the water begins to boil. Reduce heat and simmer fruit, uncovered, for 15 minutes. Drain the fruit and set aside to cool.

While the fruit is cooling, roll out the pastry dough and fit it into tartlet tins, 3½ inches × ¾ inch, or two 8-inch loose-bottomed tart rings. Peel and core the apples and chop fine. Place the orange or apple juice, brown sugar and brandy in a large bowl and whisk to blend. Stir in the cooled dried fruit, chopped pecans and apple until well combined.

Preheat oven to 450°F. Arrange the tart pans on a large baking sheet. Fill each pastry shell with approximately ⅓ cup of filling, or divide the filling between the two 8-inch tarts. Bake for 10 minutes, then reduce oven temperature to 350°F. Bake for 35 to 45 minutes, or until the pastry is golden brown and the fruit lightly browned on top. Place on wire racks until cool enough to handle, about 20 minutes.

Carefully loosen the tartlets from tins by using the tip of a sharp knife to separate the pastry from the sides of the tins. Then carefully invert the tart pan into the palm of one hand. Press in on the bottom of the pan with the thumb of the other hand to release the bottom of the pastry shell. Lift out of the pan and carefully place tartlet right side up on a wire rack to continue cooling. Repeat with remaining tartlets. If you have made 8-inch tarts, after loosening pastry from sides of tart tins, set tins on the tops of wide-mouth jars and slip tart rings down around them, leaving tarts and bottoms of rings on top of jar. Set tarts on a rack.

To serve, arrange on a large attractive tray or platter. If desired, place a large bowl of whipped cream near the tartlets so guests can help themselves.

Gingerbread-Apple Trifle with Custard Sauce

Preparations for this dessert should begin 2 days before serving. The trifle may be assembled and served in a large—at least 4-quart capacity—cut glass or other attractive serving bowl. The top can be garnished with whipped cream, and sprinkled with finely chopped crystallized ginger. Or, if you prefer, the trifle can be assembled in a large bowl with a very narrow base and then turned out to make an attractive dome-shaped trifle. Spread the outside of the trifle with a layer of whipped cream and then decorate with whipped cream piped in a diamond pattern, sprinkled with finely chopped crystallized ginger. If the trifle is unmolded, cut it into wedges for serving rather than spooning it out of a large serving bowl, as you do in the first presentation.

25 portions

1	recipe Custard Sauce with Crystallized Ginger (recipe follows)
1	recipe Brown Sugar Gingerbread (recipe follows)
4½	pounds firm apples, such as Granny Smith, Rome Beauty or Golden Delicious
1	lemon
4	tablespoons unsalted butter
4	tablespoons sugar
1	cup heavy cream, chilled
¼	cup finely chopped crystallized ginger

Two days before serving, make the custard sauce, cover, and refrigerate. On the same day make the gingerbread. When thoroughly cooled, cut the gingerbread in half horizontally, so that you have 4 layers, each approximately 1 inch thick. Let stand overnight, uncovered, on wire racks so that it will dry out. This is important as it will keep the trifle from becoming too soggy.

One day before serving, quarter and peel the apples and cut into ¼-inch slices. You should have about 10 cups. Grate the yellow rind of the lemon to measure 1 teaspoon. Heat 2 tablespoons of the butter in a large heavy saucepan over medium-high heat. When the foam begins to subside, add half of the apple slices. Sauté over high heat, stirring frequently and shaking the skillet until apples begin to brown. Sprinkle with 2 tablespoons of the sugar and ½ teaspoon of the lemon rind. Continue to sauté over high heat, stirring the apples and shaking the skillet, until the apples just begin to caramelize. Quickly remove from the heat and turn out onto a large platter to cool. Repeat with the remaining butter, apples, sugar and lemon rind. Leave apples at room temperature to cool thoroughly.

Reserve 2 cups of the custard sauce for serving time. From the approximately 2 cups that remain, ladle just enough sauce to form a very thin coating on the bottom of the serving bowl. Tear or cut enough gingerbread to fit in a single layer in the bottom of the bowl. Spread one third of the apples over the gingerbread layer. Drizzle with one quarter of the remaining custard sauce. Repeat layering of the gingerbread, apples and custard sauce twice more, ending with a layer of gingerbread lightly drizzled with custard sauce. If you have been a little too generous with the custard sauce, you may have to borrow a couple of tablespoons from the portion reserved for serving time. Place a piece of plastic wrap directly on the top layer of gingerbread and cover it with a plate, just large enough to fit directly on the top layer of gingerbread and to weight the trifle gently. Refrigerate the trifle overnight to allow the flavors to mellow.

Whip the heavy cream until stiff. Decorate the unmolded trifle or the top of the trifle in the bowl with a diamond-shaped pattern of piped whipped cream. Sprinkle with the crystallized ginger. Serve with a pitcher of the reserved custard sauce.

Brown Sugar Gingerbread

makes 2 layers, 13 × 9 inches

½	pound unsalted butter
1	cup packed dark brown sugar
2	eggs
2	cups molasses
4½	cups all-purpose flour
2	tablespoons ground ginger
1	tablespoon baking soda
1	teaspoon ground cloves
½	teaspoon salt
2	cups boiling water

Lightly butter two baking pans, each 13 × 9 inches. Sprinkle with flour and tap out excess. Preheat oven to 350°F.

In the bowl of an electric mixer or by hand, cream the butter and sugar together until light and fluffy. Add the eggs, one at a time, beating well after each addition. Gradually beat in the molasses until thoroughly blended.

Sift the flour, ginger, baking soda, cloves and salt onto a large sheet of wax paper. Little by little, add to the butter mixture, beating each addition just until blended.

Very gradually, add the boiling water, stirring constantly and carefully by hand with a large mixing spoon and making sure the water is incorporated as you add it. Divide the batter evenly between the prepared baking pans. Bake for about 45 minutes, or until the cake has pulled away from the sides of the pans and the center is firm to the touch.

Cool the cakes, in their pans, on wire racks. Turn out and continue to cool until ready to use.

Custard Sauce with Crystallized Ginger

makes about 4½ cups

10	egg yolks
⅔	cup sugar
4	cups half-and-half

¼	cup finely chopped crystallized ginger
1	teaspoon vanilla extract

Place the egg yolks and sugar in the top of a double boiler and beat about 5 minutes, or until thick and lemon-colored.

Meanwhile, heat the half-and-half in a separate saucepan until very hot but not boiling. Very gradually, stir the hot half-and-half into the yolk mixture until thoroughly blended. Cook the mixture over hot, but not boiling, water, being sure the bottom of the egg yolk pan does not touch the water. Stir constantly for about 20 minutes, until the custard thickens enough to coat the back of a metal spoon. Pour the sauce into a bowl and set aside to cool slightly, stirring frequently. Stir in the ginger and vanilla. Leave at room temperature until thoroughly cool. Refrigerate, covered, until ready to use.

INDEX